EVE'S
SECRETS

Eve's Secrets

A New Theory of Female Sexuality

by

JOSEPHINE
LOWNDES SEVELY

RANDOM HOUSE
New York

Library of Congress Cataloging-in-Publication Data

Sevely, Josephine Lowndes.
Eve's secrets.

Bibliography: p.
1. Sex (Biology)   2. Sex (Psychology)
I. Title.
QP251.S476   1987   306.7   86-31366
ISBN 0-394-55438-8

ACKNOWLEDGMENTS

To my family, whose understanding support has sustained me through the past decade's work, my deepest gratitude. I am also deeply thankful to the friends and colleagues who through their help, discussions of ideas, and expressions of confidence in the importance of my research have been a source of encouragement over the years. I have been especially fortunate to have had among my earliest supporters George Goethals, who, recognizing the potential significance of my work at an early stage, supervised my studies at Harvard; and John Money, at Johns Hopkins, who listened with open mind and interest to the ideas I had developed concerning the female fluids and helped to get published my Harvard paper on the subject. I feel a sense of personal debt to the educational and medical institutions that shared their facilities so generously in the course of my research and writing—most of all Harvard for having opened its vast resources to me. It should go without saying, but is customary to make clear, that although I acknowledge the many contributions of others to this work, in no way should they or their institutions be thought to be responsible for my ideas or for the way in which I chose to present those ideas.

The women who participated as subjects must remain anonymous, but these acknowledgments would not be complete without a recognition of their generosity in volunteering to contribute to these studies.

((v))

ACKNOWLEDGMENTS

I am grateful to Anne Freedgood, my editor at Random House, for her professional judgment in guiding me in the writing of *Eve's Secrets,* for her incisive criticism and sensitivity to the integrity of the work, and for her dedication to its success from our very first meeting.

I wish to thank Morty Schiff for the many ideas he contributed in the writing of the manuscript.

My thanks go also to Robert Gottlieb and Daniel Strone, my agents at William Morris, for their many suggestions and for their confidence in the book from its first presentation to them in its embryonic form.

I also have the good fortune as an author to have the wise counsel of Robert Duggan, of Palmer and Dodge.

Through this book I am pleased to share with readers some of the very rare and invaluable texts and illustrations at the Harvard Countway Library of Medicine. I wish to thank Richard Wolfe, Curator of Rare Books and Manuscripts, Joseph Garland Librarian of the Boston Medical Library, for making this possible, as well as the members of his staff for their courteous help over years.

Some chapters in this book are heavily illustrated, including original work sensitively rendered by the Cambridge design organization Graphix.

As John Donne reminds us in his *Devotions,* "No man is an island, entire of it self;" so, finally, I wish to pay tribute to the women and men of the 1920s, among them members of my immediate family, the courageous scientists of that period, especially the gynecologist Robert Latou Dickinson, and the friends I came to love—some now long deceased—whose spirit and idealism have contributed so much to my own generation.

CONTENTS

*S*ex is a *private* and very personal affair, but people's attitudes toward it are heavily influenced by outside opinion. Society, religion, and science have all presented us with dogmas that strongly affect the dynamics of our lovemaking. Preconceived ideas—some of them hundreds of years old—about the superiority of the male gender or the roles men and women should play still condition our sexual lives and expectations.

In the nineteenth century, whose influence lies heavily on our own, the female sex was divided into two types: "angels" and fallen women. The sexless woman was the ideal, and anyone who did not live up to it was thought to be a sinner.

In 1906 an outspoken physician named Joseph Richardson Parke wrote:

> Those who desire to more intimately analyze the sexual status of woman will find that, heretofore, two very opposite currents of opinion prevailed respecting it, both of which were equally false. One made woman an angel, a wholly supernatural element in human life, and the other regarded her as a mere plaything of the animal appetite, with no thought, feeling, nor purpose, outside the sexual sphere.*

The classical view of doubleness in the female sex was paralleled by a traditional double standard

*Joseph Richardson Parke, *Human Sexuality; a medico-lit-*

for the sexual behavior of men and women. Premarital sex was unthinkable for respectable women; for males, it was accepted without question. Literature on the subject spans the century. In 1809 an anonymous male author writing of the perils of female unchastity advised his readers:

> From [this] picture of unchastity . . . you may perceive, Christian Virgins, to what an abyss of spiritual and temporal miseries it plunges those who practice it. How careful then ought you to be in guarding all avenues that lead to it, such as loose discourses, books, pastimes, touches, caresses, embraces, gallantries, privacies, and a thousand other causes which to you may seem but so many innocent amusements, but which too often and too assuredly pave the way to great inconveniences in this life, and terminate in torments in the next.*

For women to work on the necessary plan of acquiring and preserving their husband's esteem, the author further advised:

> You must first lay it down for a foundation in general that there is an inequality in the sexes, and that for the economy of the world, the men who were to be guardians and lawgivers had not only the greater share of bodily strength bestowed on them, but those also of reason and resolution.

---

erary treatise on the laws, anomalies, and relations of sex, with especial reference to contrary sexual desire . . . (Philadelphia: Professional Publishing Company, 1906), p. 224.

*The Female Friend; or the Duties of Christian Virgins to which is added, Advice to a Young Married Lady. By F . . . . . . L . . . . . ., Esq. (Baltimore: Henry S. Keatinge, 1809), p. 48.

Your sex will be the better prepared from this necessary reflection for the compliance and passiveness that may be required and is necessary for the better performance of those duties which seem to be most properly assigned to it by nature.*

Eduard von Hartmann (1842–1906), author of *Philosophy of the Unconscious* (1867), also wrote *The Sexes Compared and Other Essays,* which was translated from the original German into English in 1895. In the translator's words, Hartmann makes clear a fundamental distinction between the sexes that "separates them by an impassable gulf":

It is a distinction between activity and passivity, of desiring and satisfying, of wooing and being wooed. . . . If both were active, then too much preponderance would be given to the sexual side of life. If both were passive, Nature's aim would not be sufficiently secured. . . . The virginity of the bride is therefore a *sine qua non* of the marriage ceremony, and every deception on that point should, like adultery, form a legal ground for divorce. If, on the contrary, the chastity of the bridegroom were indispensable to matrimony, then, generally speaking, only such men would rear legitimate families whose physiological shortcomings would scarcely make their multiplication desirable. . . . A man may marry a widow but the woman has to make her "widowhood" clear to the man and must deserve this favor by extraordinary personal charms. A maiden, on the other hand, who enters into nuptial relations with a widower loses nothing by the bargain. She may, indeed, heartily congratulate herself on being

*Ibid., p. 174.

united to a man already civilized and tamed by her predecessor.*

On the subject of the difference between the once-engaged man and woman, Hartmann wrote:

> The former's value is in no way affected as long as the betrothal was broken off through no fault of his own. The latter, even if her conduct were absolutely irreproachable, would be like an article of merchandise spoiled by shipwreck and consequently fallen in price. However strictly she may have maintained her womanly passivity during her engagement, it is no longer latent. . . . The virginity of her heart is no longer "intact." The fragrance has departed from the rose.†

In 1894 the Reverend L. E. Keith, writing under the pseudonym Feelix Feeler, discussed the age of consent for girls, which he believed should not be raised but erased altogether, reasoning that if the moral standards of his times were to be elevated, both sexes should be chaste. He bemoaned the double standard and the fact that women as well as men accepted it as normal practice: "Chastity is an absolute essential in a woman . . . but it is not essential in men. How often do we hear men, and women too, say 'Oh, boys must sow their wild oats. They will settle down all right after a while and make excellent husbands.' "‡ In Europe there may have been more sex-

*Eduard von Hartmann, *The Sexes Compared and Other Essays,* translated by A. Kenner (London: Swan Sonnenschein and Company; New York: Macmillan and Co., 1895), pp. 1, 10, 11.
†Ibid., p. 14.
‡Rev. L. E. Keith, (Feelix Feeler), *Female Filosophy: Fished Out and Fried* (1894), p. 256. Sterling Memorial Library, Yale University.

ual openness in print—in 1886 the German scientist R. von Krafft-Ebing, for example, published *Psychopathia Sexualis*—but there, too, attitudes about the sexuality of women held fast to the view that the sexual impulse was much stronger in men than in women and that for men love was largely sensual, whereas in women sexual desire was considered to be normally at a very low level. A woman, it was thought, yielded to the coital act as a duty or as a favor to her husband.

"According to the standard view of women's sexuality in the nineteenth century," historian Carl Degler reported in 1974, "women were not expected to feel desire and certainly not to experience an orgasm."* Dr. William Acton, an authority writing in the 1850s, succinctly stated the current attitudes: "The majority of women (happily for them) are not very much troubled with sexual feelings of any kind. What men are habitually, women are only exceptionally."†

Degler also cited an article that described the general view of physicians in the 1800s:‡ "Male doctors were so convinced that women had no sexual interest that when it manifested itself, drastic mea-

---

*Carl Degler, "What Ought to Be and What Was: Women's Sexuality in the Nineteenth Century," *American Historical Review,* December 1974, p. 1483.

†William Acton, *The Functioning and Disorders of the Reproductive Organs in Youth, in Adult Age, and in Advanced Life: Considered in Their Physiological, Social, and Psychological Relations* (London, 1857; Philadelphia, 1865), p. 133. Quoted in Degler, *op. cit.,* pp. 1467–8.

‡Ben Barker-Benfield, "The Spermatic Economy: A Nineteenth Century View of Sexuality," *Feminist Studies,* 1:54, 1972. Quoted in Degler, *op. cit.,* p. 1468.

sures were taken to subdue it, including excision of the sexual organs." Doctors of the period defined the absence of sexual desire in women as normal and saw any evidence of its presence as disease. "Sexual appetite was a male quality (to be properly channeled of course)," the article reports. "If a woman showed it, she resembled a man."

Degler believes that the Victorian stereotype was more theoretical than actual; that because of the reticence about sex in the excessively genteel middle class, fallacious impressions about sexual reality took hold. He concludes that the nature of what was written about sex was prescriptive rather than descriptive, or, at least, a mixture of the two.

Nineteenth-century women may have publicly appeared to embrace the idea of female sexlessness, but the dictate of the culture "to lie still and think of the Empire," as recommended by one British authority, was not a sexual fate acceptable to all. In an 1894 article, Dr. Elizabeth Blackwell challenged the notion that sexual passion was stronger in men than in women. In her view, to assess qualities of males and females as separate was a futility. She warned of the social disturbances that can stem from the thwarting in women of the vital force of human sex.*

Nevertheless, as late as 1947, women were still being characterized as sexually passive. Authors Ferdinand Lundberg and Marynia F. Farnham, while sympathetic to the plight of women who had to deal with repressive societal attitudes, wrote: "It is

*Elizabeth Blackwell, "Sexual Passion in Men and Women" (1894), in Nancy Cott, ed., *Roots of Bitterness: Documents of the Social History of American Women* (New York: Dutton, 1972), pp. 299–303.

not as easy as rolling off a log for her [woman]. It is easier. It is as easy as being the log itself."*

Marie Bonaparte, one of the leading twentieth-century authorities on female sexuality, wrote in 1953:

> Woman offers us not a few enigmas and, in especial, this apparent contradiction; on the one hand, as we saw in all we have so far related, she generally seems less well endowed than man to achieve her erotic destiny, less charged with libido and more fettered in functional adaptation to it than he is; on the other, it is generally said, and apparently with reason, that woman is more instinctive and more deeply embedded in sexuality, often to the exclusion of all else.†

In the first half of the twentieth century, the age-old idea of sexual dichotomy in the female expressed itself in the notion that respectable women were innocent and virginal before marriage and sexually passive as wives, while only besmirched, worldly women enjoyed sex. The "flappers" of the twenties, who cut their hair and their skirts short, wore obvious makeup, smoked cigarettes, drank along with men, and showed their legs, shocked the sensibilities of conventional Americans, who looked upon them as "loose" women. Though men and women lived together out of wedlock, the practice was usually clandestine and universally described as "living in sin."

*Ferdinand Lundberg, and Marynia F. Farnham, *Modern Woman: The Lost Sex* (New York: Harper & Brothers, 1947), p. 275.

†Marie Bonaparte, *Female Sexuality* (New York: International Universities Press, 1953), p. 67.

Young adults in the 1980s may find it hard to imagine how abrupt and recent the change in societal attitudes about female sexuality has actually been. In the wake of taboos, suppression, and denial, attitudes about the sexuality of women underwent a revolution, but this did not occur in the United States until the late 1960s and early 1970s.

Today there is a concentration on sex differences and, at the same time, on the fact that the responses involved in sexual arousal and orgasm are not that different in the male and the female. Thanks to the pioneering research of Alfred Kinsey and later of William Masters and Virginia Johnson, we now know that men and women are equally arousable by tactile stimulation and have the same neural and muscular responses. In fact, their muscles contract during orgasm at the same precise 0.8-second interval. Nevertheless, women are still popularly supposed to need more physical stimulation than men and to play a generally secondary role in the sex act.

This book is an outgrowth of my own questioning of this theory of female sexuality. I was trained in psychology, and I am accustomed to evaluating evidence dispassionately. If all orgasms are the same, why, I asked myself, are men's orgasms supposed to be objective and women's subjective? Then I began to think about the apparently unassailable pronouncement that the only phenomenon in the physiology of sexual response not identically matched in men and women is ejaculation: men ejaculate, women do not. I began to question this premise, for in my reading I was constantly coming across references to female fluids.

Unfortunately, these were initially for the most

part negative references to the relationship between female fluids and genital disorders. For example, in *Dora: A Case of Hysteria,* Sigmund Freud describes some of Dora's symptoms, which included genital secretions that were viewed as abnormal. Apparently, doctors used to believe that there was a correlation between the two conditions; women whose hysterical condition worsened also often "suffered" symptoms of increased genital secretions. Writing in a more general vein on the subject, Freud addressed some of the psychological aspects:

> The pride taken by women in the appearance of their genitals is quite a special feature of their vanity; and disorders of the genitals which they think calculated to inspire feelings of repugnance or even disgust have an incredible power of humiliating them, of lowering their self-esteem, and of making them irritable, sensitive, and distrustful. An abnormal secretion of the mucous membrane of the vagina is looked upon as a source of disgust.*

But the Kinsey reports had alerted me to the fact that there was widespread folk knowledge about female ejaculation, and other readings had taught me about the open acceptance of the phenomenon in other cultures in earlier times when awareness of "female semen," also called "female fecund fluids," was part of scientific and popular belief. The belief usually had to do with reproduction, not sex; but

*Sigmund Freud, "Fragment of an Analysis of a Case of Hysteria" (1905 [1901]), in *The Standard Edition of the Complete Psychological Works by Sigmund Freud,* Vol. VII, trans. and ed. by James Strachey (London: The Hogarth Press and the Institute of Psycho-Analysis, 1953), p. 84.

tracking down more detailed descriptions of the fecund fluids, I found one scientist who had not failed to notice their erotic nature. In a major work describing the generative organs of women, Regnier de Graaf in 1672 made the connection between the fluids and female sexual pleasure. If women in the seventeenth century had normally experienced a sexual response that women in the twentieth century were not supposed to have, then, I thought, something had to be amiss.

Actually, the germ of this book was planted a decade ago when, as a graduate student at Harvard, I decided to take a tutorial that offered students an opportunity to devote time to independent research on a topic of their own choice. Drawing upon my interest in theories of female sexuality and an undergraduate paper I had written on women, sexuality, and the female ejaculate, I submitted a proposal to study the subject of female sexual fluids in scientific literature and to reexamine the prevailing assumption that women did not ejaculate. The result was a lengthy manuscript, "Female Ejaculation," a summary of which appeared as an article in 1978 in *The Journal of Sex Research* under the title "Concerning Female Ejaculation and the Female Prostate." I concluded that women do ejaculate and urged members of the scientific community to conduct further research.

Soon afterward, I set up a privately funded research organization in Cambridge, Massachusetts, to conduct studies on issues relevant to women and their interpersonal relationships. Foremost among its objectives was women's health and the study of female sexual fluids, including their possible implications for the reproductive process.

In the summer of 1979, I visited the Department of Obstetrics and Gynecology at Brigham and Women's Hospital to see if it would be possible to have the necessary laboratory analyses done through the department. In the series of meetings that followed, I presented the work I had done and a proposal for studies designed to characterize the fluids, which studies I was able to begin to implement in 1981.

In the selection of participants, special attention was given to the guidelines of the American Psychological Association Ethical Principles in the Conduct of Research with Human Subjects (1973). The procedures and required consent form were approved and reviewed annually by the Committee for the Protection of Human Subjects from Research Risks of the Hospital from 1982 to 1985, and were also approved by the Institutional Review Board of the Harvard Medical School Committee on Human Studies in 1983 and 1984. The statements and opinions expressed in this book, however, are those of the author and not necessarily those of any members of the above institutions. Neither the various specialists who have helped me in the course of the work nor their institutions should be thought to endorse the results of the investigations.

In order to understand the physiological mechanisms involved in the production of the fluids, one has to have a thorough knowledge of the relevant anatomy. For this reason, over the next few years the research included a study of the female urethra and vagina. Through the knowledge gained thereby, I was able to discern a relationship between the female and male sexual anatomy that was at variance with the established theory of male and female counterparts. Before presenting my idea, I studied all I could find about the embryological differentiation of the sexes and the adult male sexual anatomy, through which I obtained more evidence that supported my new direction of thought.

The theory of male and female counterparts that had been accepted for so many centuries did not, I began to realize, develop as part of the normal scientific process. It was based on preconceptions about the sexes that went back to the ancient Greeks' and early Judaic/Christian writers' notions of sexual inequality and of woman as an incomplete version of man. I was able to trace these ideas not only in philosophy and religion but in early Western medical texts. The physicians who first described the female genitals—who were, of course, all men—described them from the same male point of view, as an inferior version of the male's.

I began looking at the accepted theory of the female anatomy, subjecting it to reevaluation in light of a different perspective, and then, step by step, as I was able to fit the pieces of the puzzle together, adding new information about the male sexual anatomy as well as the female's. The way in which my theory developed is not too different from the usual process, but the time frame was unusual. We have become accustomed to new ideas in a specific field at least once a decade, but in the case of the female sexual anatomy, there had not been any basic change for twenty centuries.

Scientific study normally has more than one dimension. There are, traditionally, scientists who test hypotheses in the laboratory within an accepted theory and add to data, and theoreticians who introduce a whole new orientation required for new understanding of familiar data. New concepts, especially those that fly in the face of long-entrenched ideas, are bound to encounter resistance. Stephen Jay Gould, the scientist recently under attack for his revision of Darwin's theory of evolution, cites the nineteenth-century naturalist Louis Agassiz, who made the following observation: "First people say it isn't true; then that it is against religion; and, in the third stage, that it has long been known."

New theories are not assimilated and accepted overnight, nor can they be proven overnight by a simple confirmation or falsification one-step process. As Thomas Kuhn recognizes,* it is only the historical process of competition in the scientific community that ever actually results in the rejection of one previously accepted theory or in the adoption of another. Kuhn is also aware that the invention of new theories evokes resistance from some of the specialists on whose area of competence they impinge. For these scientists, Kuhn points out, the new theory implies a change in the rules governing the prior practice of normal science. Inevitably, therefore, it reflects upon much scientific work they have already successfully completed. Ernst Mayr, a scientist who has written about the development of ideas, also

*Thomas S. Kuhn, *The Structure of Scientific Revolutions,* Vol. II, No. 2 (Chicago: The University of Chicago Press, 1970), pp. viii, ix, 7.

recognizes that a new theory will inevitably engender a certain resistance.* It implies a change in the rules with which others have come to be comfortable; and for scientists, since it reflects on work already done, necessitates the rejection of a time-honored way of thinking about something in favor of another incompatible with that way. For these reasons, I knew that before I presented my ideas they had to be backed up by sound logical reasoning and consistency of argument in my interpretation of the facts and adaptation of the work of responsible authorities.

The development of my own ideas relied heavily on the work of scientists whose publications contributed to our knowledge of anatomy and various other specialized medical fields pertinent to my topic. Sources of material are listed in the Bibliography at the back of this book. Among the many works I found helpful were those of Robert Latou Dickinson, Milo H. Spaulding, Kermit E. Krantz, A. B. Huisman, and the contributors to *The Human Vagina,* edited by E.S.E. Hafez and T. N. Evans.

Finally in 1984 I felt ready to discuss my theory with colleagues, whose support and advice both as physicians and rigorous devil's advocates played a vital role in my work. It is my hope that the insight gained from this new perspective of male and female urogenital homologues will be of interest to clinicians and researchers more broadly, and that it will engender greater recognition of the need for gener-

*Ernst Mayr, *The Growth of Biological Thought: Diversity, Evolution, and Inheritance* (Cambridge, Mass.: Harvard University Press, 1982).

ous funding in the future of further characterization of the female sexual fluids and of investigation of the potentially significant reproductive aspects of this research. I also hope that the new theory may prompt embryologists to start thinking in different ways from the past about the problem of sexual differentiation and to recognize that questions about the development of the urogenital system remain to be resolved. I recognize that there is still much more research to be done, but, in the process of the work accomplished to date, significant discoveries have been made about the anatomy that are important to bring immediately to the attention of the general public. For this reason, I decided to publish the present overall research findings in book form. Their significance is, I hope, obvious. To discover in explicit detail how much alike they are sexually should help men and women to understand both themselves and each other better. The new theory offers women for the first time a way of perceiving how men relate to *them* sexually instead of vice versa; it offers men a new awareness of their own sexual anatomy and a greater insight into what it is that excites and pleases women sexually. With such knowledge, couples will be able to achieve a broader range of possibilities for mutual pleasure and pleasuring. Beyond its sexual implications, this book provides a basis for a new kind of dialogue compatible with the sense of shared identity and closeness most lovers feel in moments of intense, intimate passion.

JOSEPHINE LOWNDES SEVELY
New York, New York
June 1986

EVE'S
SECRETS

FIG. 1 Studies of a Man and a Woman (*Jean Auguste Dominique Ingres, "The Golden Age," 1780–1867*)

CHAPTER 1

The Lowndes Crowns Theory

For centuries science has contended that the clitoris is a female organ that corresponds to the penis of the male. If you look in the 1981 unabridged edition of Webster's Third New International Dictionary, you will find the clitoris defined as "a small organ at the anterior or ventral part of the vulva homologous to the penis in the male." The prevailing scientific theory of homologues, or counterparts, also contends that the tip of the clitoris corresponds to the tip of the penis. For this reason, both these male and female parts have been called the glans, a Greek word meaning "acorn."

There are, of course, some similarities between the penile glans and the clitoral glans: both are visible, external parts; both are located in the genital area; both indeed are outermost tips; and both are erotically sensitive to tactile stimulation.

As far back as 1672, however, the Dutch anatomist Regnier de Graaf raised some questions about the theory. To a perceptive anatomist like de Graaf, the conspicuous difference in the sizes of the two organs was not the most significant factor. He made more fundamental arguments against the idea: "Unlike the penis, the clitoris has no urethra or similar channel." And since the glans of the clitoris is not perforated like that of the penile glans, he reasoned that "its similarity to the male glans is thus deceptive."* Yet, even though the differences between the two are a lot greater than their similarities, de Graaf did not actually discredit the already entrenched penis/clitoris idea.

Only now do we have sufficient knowledge to challenge the theory. Although I uphold the validity of the ancient approach of identifying counterparts, I believe that the penis/clitoris analogy is wrong. I intend to show that this notion came about in a rather unusual way as the result of two things: a biased perspective that interfered with the rational process normally associated with science, and bad translations of ancient anatomical texts that distorted original meanings.

The word "homologue" is derived from the Greek *homologia,* meaning agreement. Originally, anatomists identified counterparts simply by visual observation of an agreement in form between two parts. The idea of homologues has its roots in the ideas of the ancient Greek philosophers, who thought in terms of an archetype, or perfect form, followed by a descending hierarchy of less-than-perfect forms.

Plato introduced the idea of a hierarchal order in

*Regnier de Graaf, *New Treatise Concerning the Generative Organs of Women,* 24, 1672. English translation by H. D. Jocelyn and B. P. Setchell, in *Journal of Reproduction and Fertility,* Supplement 17 (Oxford: Blackwell Scientific Publications, 1972), p. 91.

nature based on intelligence, with man at the top followed by other two-legged creatures (woman included), then quadrupeds, snakes, down the chain to fish. Aristotle, a student of Plato, incorporated this same idea in his own thinking and developed a hierarchy of genus-species classifications arranged in order of "perfection," a quality that he equated with heat. Since the human species was above all others, and since he decided that the male of the human species was hotter than the female, he put man at the top of the hierarchy, followed by the relatively colder woman, so on down the line, with the cold fish last. As I will show later, his writings also reveal the assumption that women are, at best, of lukewarm intelligence.

An understanding of the philosophical underpinnings of the homologue idea helps to clarify the medical outlook. When the early anatomists first identified certain sexual parts in males and females as counterparts based on likeness in form, they did so from the Aristotelian outlook of a hierarchal order in which the female was perceived as inferior to the male.

Early Christian scientists who dealt with the identification of anatomical parts were influenced by the Holy Scriptures as well, and they contained two completely different, seemingly contradictory views on the subject of the two sexes.

"And the rib, which the Lord God had taken from man, made he a woman and brought her unto the man. And Adam said, This is now bone of my bones, and flesh of my flesh: she shall be called Woman, because she was taken out of Man" (Genesis 2:22, 23).

But Jesus asked the Pharisees, "Have ye not read

that 'he which made them at the beginning made them male and female'?" (Matthew 19:4). And if you look in Genesis (1:27), you will see that it indeed says, "So God created man in his own image, in the image of God created he him; male and female created he them."

Scholars who study the Bible can detect four different strands of writing style.* The rib version in Genesis 2 is attributed to writers who referred to God by the name of Jahweh (Jehova), called Jahwists. The idea of woman in Genesis 1—which, in my opinion, is suggestive of equality of the sexes—is attributed to Jewish priests. The Priestly version, as it is called, says, "male and female created he *them.*" The use of "them" is significant, for it conveys the meaning that God made both Adam and Eve out of the earth—not man first out of earth and woman later out of bone.

Early Christian physicians, too, began to say two things at the same time: "Woman is made in man's image," but "The female body is an inferior version of the male's." The idea, reinforcing as it was of the Greek notion, came to prevail that although each part of the female anatomy is a counterpart of one in the male anatomy, the female counterparts, because they were derived from the male, were secondary and, therefore, inferior. The early theory of counterparts was the foundation upon which we have built the superstructure of human anatomy: the male parts first and then the derivative female parts.

*Northrop Frye, *The Great Code: The Bible and Literature* (New York: Harcourt, Brace, Jovanovich, 1983), p. 107. The four traditions of Biblical writings are: Jahwists, Priestly, Elolists, and Deuteronomists.

Galen (A.D. 129–c. 199), the Greek-born physician whose authority dominated ancient medicine, introduced the idea that the vagina was the counterpart of the penis. Galen, who came to be known in Rome as "the wonder worker," described a woman's vagina as "a penis turned inside out" (Figure 2), an idea that may at first glance appear somewhat whimsical, but which was, as I will show in a later chapter, indeed insightful.

Galen practiced in a time when scientists faced severe restrictions on their work imposed by philosophical attitudes about the sexes and societal prohibitions. When, for example, Galen describes the female genitals as a "mutilated" version of the male's, he is reflecting the general assumption of his era that man was superior to woman:

> Now just as mankind is the most perfect of all animals, so within mankind the man is more perfect than the woman. . . . The woman is less perfect than the man in respect to the generative parts. . . . Indeed, you ought not to think that our Creator would purposely make half the whole race imperfect and, as it were, mutilated, unless there was to be some great advantage in such mutilation.*

Since examination of the female genitals was left for the most part to midwives, Galen had limited opportunity in his practice to observe women's "shameful parts." Furthermore, dissection of human corpses was outlawed. The only way Galen could ob-

*Galen, *On the Usefulness of the Parts* (Bk. 14.6), Vol. II, trans. by Margaret Tallmadge May (Ithaca, N.Y.: Cornell University Press, 1968), p. 630.

DE HVMANI CORPORIS FABRICA LIBER V.
VIGESIMA·SEPTIMA QVINTI
LIBRI FIGVRA.

PRÆSENS *figura uterum*
à corpore exectum ea magnitudine re-
fert, qua postremò Patauij dissectæ
mulieris uterus nobis occurrit. atq; ut
uteri circunscriptionem hic expressi-
mus,ita etiam ipsius fundum per mediũ
dissecuimus, ut illius sinus in conspe-
ctum ueniret, una cum ambarum uteri
tunicarũ in non prægnantibus substan-
tiæ crassitie.

A, A. B, B Vteri fundi sinus.

C,D *Linea quodãmodo instar suturæ, qua*
scortum donatur,in uteri fundi sinum le
uiter protuberans.

E,E *Interioris ac propriæ fundi uteri tuni*
cæ crassities.

F,F *Interioris fundi uteri portio,ex elatio*
ri uteri sede deorsum in fundi sinũ pro-
tuberans.

G,G *Fundi uteri orificium.*

H,H *Secundum exteriusq̃; fundi uteri inuo-*
lucrum,à peritonæo pronatum.

I,I *et c. Membranarum à peritonæo pro*
natarum, & uterum continentium por
tionem utrinq̃; hic asseruauimus.

K *Vteri ceruicis substantia hic quoque*
conspicitur, quod sectio qua uteri fun-
dum diuisimus,inibi incipiebatur.

L *Vesicæ ceruicis pars,uteri cēruici in-*
serta,ac urinam in illam proijciens.
Vteri colles, & si quid hic spectãdam
sit reliqui,etiam nullis appositis chara
cteribus,nulli non patent.

§ VIGE-

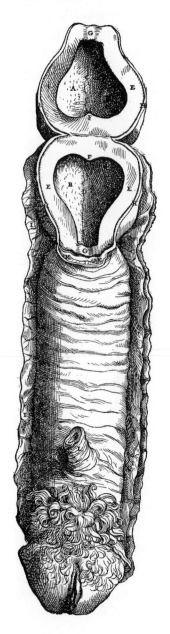

FIG. 2 Human Vagina
(*Vesalius*, Fabrica, 1543)

tain knowledge about the female anatomy was by dissecting female pigs and monkeys. Nevertheless, despite these restrictions and limitations, Galen was able to come up with the penis/vagina idea, and emphatically stated that the only difference between the male and female parts was that the female genitals are inside the body and those of the male outside (Box 1). Therefore he reasoned that if the penis is turned inside out, it will become the vagina, and the foreskin will become the skin that is the appendage to the vagina. By appendage, Galen meant the skin that forms the inner folds.* Nothing is said in Galen's

---

1 GALEN

All the male genital parts are also found in women. There is not any difference except for one point...that is, that the female parts are internal and those of the male are external, taking their origin in the region called the perineum.

Suppose these parts of the male are turned inside out and, at the same time, on the inside extend themselves between the rectum and the bladder. Within this hypothesis, the scrotum will necessarily occupy the place of the vagina, with the ovaries situated at each side in the fashion of the external portion; the penis of the male becomes the passageway that the hollow creates, and the part situated at the tip of the penis, now called "prepuce," becomes the external genital parts of the woman.

Galen, *De usu part.* Lib. XIV, second century A.D.

---

*The inner folds are officially called the *labia minora,* a Latin term meaning "little lips," which was introduced by

text about the clitoris as we know the part. He does use the Greek word *pudenda* for the external genital parts, but by no stretch of the imagination could he have intended that word to mean the part that in later times came to be called the clitoris.

For well over a thousand years, no one dared to question Galen's authority. Then the sixteenth century witnessed a renaissance in the study of anatomy, led by a handful of courageous men that included the Italian Gabriel Fallopio and his teacher, Vesalius.

Vesalius lived from 1514 to 1564. Although dissection of the human body was no longer outlawed, it was still difficult for him to get cadavers, even in his capacity as head of anatomy at the University of Padua. Of the six corpses known to be obtained by Vesalius for his studies of the female anatomy, one was not properly preserved; the remains of another—a murdered pregnant woman—had to be returned for legal proceedings; and three others were needed for public demonstrations. That left Vesalius with but one body, that of a woman who had been hanged, upon which to base his findings.

Despite the revolution in the study of anatomy brought about by these young Renaissance scientists (Vesalius was only twenty-nine years old when his major work was published), little advance was made in relation to the female genital anatomy. It was not only the lack of specimens for dissection that hindered progress. Because of the attitude of the Church that men and women should engage in coitus only as a means of creating new life, Christian physicians

---

Realdo Colombo (1516–1559); the fleshy, outer folds are called the *labia majora*.

tended to overlook those parts of the female body deemed to be irrelevant to reproduction. The focus of concern was the uterus; the female genitals were for the most part disregarded.

It is not surprising, then, that in Vesalius's major work, *Fabrica* (1543), he depicts the vagina precisely as Galen had described it (Figure 2). In over twelve centuries, virtually nothing had changed; Vesalius clearly perceived the female anatomy in the same way that Galen had.

Not so Fallopio. Younger than his teacher by only about nine years, Fallopio was bolder than Vesalius in attacking the teachings of Galen. (As a matter of fact, he corrected some of the erroneous views of Vesalius as well, having gone on to succeed Vesalius in the chair of anatomy at Padua.) Fallopio let neither the internal nor the external parts of the female anatomy escape his notice; he was the discoverer of the uterine tubes that bear his name, and he is also credited with the first detailed description of the clitoris. Published in 1561—one year before his death at age thirty-nine—it is here translated into English for the first time in Box 2.

Before Fallopio's discovery, there was evidently no official medical publication about the deeper structures of the clitoris that he had dissected. The rather puzzling thing for the modern reader is that no one, Fallopio included, seemed to notice that his statement that the clitoris corresponded to the penis refuted Galen's penis/vagina idea. Realdo Colombo, another Italian anatomist whose work was published in 1559, similarly called the clitoris a female penis. The term Colombo used was *mentula muliebris.* This fact suggests that the penis/clitoris idea was not

2 FALLOPIO

Avicenna...mentions a part positioned in the female pudendum and calls it "a penis" or rather "al bathara" [the Arabic word translated as meaning the "clitoris"]. Albucasim...calls it "the tension." It sometimes can reach a growth so remarkable in some women that they can have coitus with each other, like men fornicating. This part is still called by the Greeks the "clitoris," and from this term is still found the verb "clitorizing" used in an obscene sense.

Truly, our anatomists completely neglected it and do not even speak of it.

This small part corresponds to the male penis....

This very private part, small in size and hidden in the very fatty part of the pubis, has remained unknown to the anatomists, so that up to now from the preceding years I am the first to describe it, and if there have been others who have spoken of it or written about it, be it known that they have not heard it spoken of by me or by those who have heard me and, therefore, only for this reason, there is not a good knowledge about it.

You will easily find the end of this kind of penis in the upper part of the external pudendum, exactly where the "hanging wings" [the outer fleshy folds]...come together or where they begin.

Gabriel Fallopio, *Observationes Anatomicae* (Venice: M.A. Ulmum, 1561).

introduced by Fallopio, but was already an accepted concept.

How *did* the penis/clitoris idea come about? A painstaking scrutiny of medical texts that span the intervening fourteen hundred years between Fallopio and Galen reveals that a seemingly inconsequential little slip was made in the translations of some early texts that resulted in a confusion of some magnitude. As the relevant texts were translated from Greek into Latin, from Latin into Arabic, then back again from Arabic into Latin, somehow the clitoris/penis idea got locked into medical thinking, and it was never questioned because everyone apparently believed that the idea represented the word of Galen—everyone, even including Fallopio, who was otherwise one of Galen's critics.

Linguists accept that there usually has to be a reason for the meaning of words to change but have learned the futility of trying to pin down precisely how the change comes about. And this case is no exception. One cannot say exactly how things got so confused, but out of the maze of semantic confusion, the following three excerpts can be selected from early texts, which, properly translated, prove that the early Greek and Arabic physicians never meant that the clitoris and penis were counterparts of each other.

1. Avicenna (Ali Ibn Sina) was the great compiler of medical knowledge that existed up to the year A.D. 1000. He himself lived from A.D. 980 to 1037. It is through his work that we know about Galen's ideas. In Avicenna's text *Of the Vagina,* he merely described each of the counterparts exactly as Galen had described them: the penis becomes the vagina; the scrotum turns into the outer folds; and the foreskin becomes the woman's external parts (the inner folds), called by Avicenna "the foreskin of the vagina."

2. Ibn Hubal (1117–1212) also upholds Galen's observation: "The inner folds are to the vaginal open-

ing what the foreskin is to the penis." Both Ibn Hubal and Avicenna use the Arabic word *al bathara,* the synonym for the Greek word "clitoris." If translated without thought to intended meaning, as was often done, Ibn Hubal's sentence would then incorrectly read: "The *clitoris* is to the vaginal opening what the foreskin is to the penis." The only part of the clitoris about which the Arabs might have known was the tip, and it would be hard to imagine the clitoral tip as a "vaginal foreskin." On the other hand, the inner folds are, in fact, recognized by physicians even in our own times as an extension of the vagina.

The Arabic physicians, and the Greeks as well, must have known about the surface part of the clitoris, because in Egypt the custom of Pharaonic circumcision—excision of the "clitoris"—was practiced, as its name suggests, quite some time back in history; but just what is excised—the tip, or the inner folds, or both—is still a matter of confusion in our own times.*

3. A clarification of all these terms exists in the work of Rufus, a first-century Greek physician who, some believe, was the physician to Cleopatra (Box 3). Rufus referred to the female external genital parts, collectively called the "pudendi," and to the "cleft," or split, that divides the outer fleshy folds. He then identified the "clitoris" as the skin that forms a woman's inner folds. This is the key to understanding.

*Today, a related confusion of terms lingers on. In the Sudan, the practice of infibulation, although forbidden by law, is still widespread. Infibulation is an operation performed on women to ensure their chastity by very direct means—removal of the external genitals, which results in a closing over of the vaginal open-

3 RUFUS

As far as the external genital parts of the woman are concerned, some refer to these as the pudendi, others as the pubis, the triangular extremity of the hypogastrium [abdomen]. The cleft is the opening of their external genital parts. The little piece of muscular flesh in its middle, called the "nymphae," also the "fruit of the myrtle," is the skin that is also named the "clitoris," and one says "clitorizing" to express the lascivious touching of this part. The "lips of the myrtle" [the outer folds] are the fleshy parts that detach themselves to each side; Euryphon names these also "the steep slopes" — today, on the one hand, one substitutes the expression "hanging wings" (pterigomata) for the outer folds, and, on the other, nymphae for the "fruit of the myrtle" [the inner folds].

Works of Rufus of Ephesus, first century A.D.

But the translators missed this clarification. To them it looked on the surface as though both the Greek and Arabic physicians were saying that the clitoris was the counterpart of the penis. If their words are interpreted not by rote repetition of literal yet incorrect translations but with respect to intended meaning, however, it becomes clear that when they used the word "clitoris," they meant the inner folds—nothing else—and, like Galen, were say-

ing with scar tissue. The midwives who perform these operations leave a reed or matchstick for the wound to heal around, so that a small opening is kept, large enough for menstrual flow but not for sexual intercourse.

Outside the Sudan, this practice is popularly known as

ing that the counterpart of the penis was the *vagina*.

Fallopio is credited with the first fully detailed description of the clitoris. He was the first to dissect its deeper internal structure—a part of the female anatomy unknown to scientists before him. In the process of making this important discovery, however, he made the error of assuming, and providing a basis for others to assume, that the clitoris was a miniature penis. The curious historical fact is that this belief came about not through valid scientific research, but as a result of an ingrained male perspective that viewed the female as inferior and an unquestioning acceptance of incorrect translations.

Even more curious is the fact that the erroneous nature of the penis/clitoris idea could have gone un-

---

"Pharaonic circumcision," and is thought by most Westerners to be removal of the tip of the clitoris only.

Many people in the West and within the cultures that practice infibulation are concerned about the women who are subjected to this form of genital mutilation. In the writings of one group of critics who want to have the practice stopped, both terms—"infibulation" and "Pharaonic circumcision"—are used interchangeably to refer to any operation that results in a closing over of the vulval area, including those operations that could involve some surgery on either the clitoral crown or the labia minora, or both. Critics of the practice recognize a distinction between two different forms of the operation—one that closes over the vulval area, and any other form of "female circumcision" that does not, such as a simple clitoridectomy (skilled removal of the clitoral crown only).

However, many of the village midwives who carry on this cultural tradition continue to reflect in practice the same lack of awareness of small variations of flesh that was evidenced in the language of the early medical writings. The language used today to describe these operations and the parts involved is still a little confusing.

detected for so many centuries. As I propose to show, an argument can be made on the basis of a reevaluation of existing anatomical facts to convincingly demonstrate that the old inadequate notion should be replaced by a new, much more plausible concept.

The new theory advanced here proposes that the clitoral tip and the penile glans are *not* counterparts of each other; the true counterparts are the female tip and the tip of a male structure *inside* the penis. The male structure is the part that fills with blood and brings about erection, a capsule-like part called the corpora cavernosa, meaning literally "cavernous bodies" (Figure 3). It can now be stated with some certainty that the true counterpart of the female clitoris is not the penis, but rather this internal part of the penis that can only be called—and that I now identify as—the male clitoris. The tips of the male and female clitorises are the Lowndes crowns, named by the author who identified the correct homology, in the tradition of anatomical parts being named by the person who makes the discovery.*

Many people may be surprised to learn that the female clitoris has deeper structures under the skin. These deeper structures are the organ's two leglike parts that run along the lower part of the pubic bones at either side of the lower vagina between the inner thighs. Simple names exist for all the parts of the clitoris: they are the crown (the tip); the corpus (the

*All the parts of the human body have been identified and named by male scientists, and many times have been named after the men themselves. To the best of my knowledge, the Lowndes crown will be the first part of the human anatomy to be named by a woman.

((17))

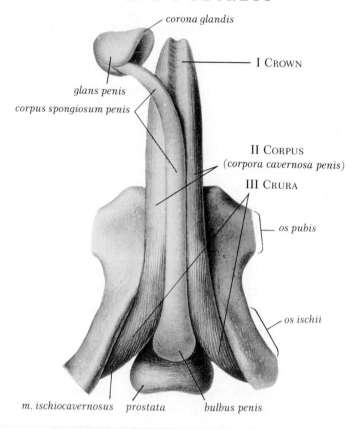

corona glandis

I CROWN

glans penis

corpus spongiosum penis

II CORPUS
(corpora cavernosa penis)

III CRURA

os pubis

os ischii

m. ischiocavernosus   *prostata*   *bulbus penis*

FIG. 3 Erectile Bodies of the Penis: glans penis and distal part of corpus spongiosum penis were lifted out of the groove in the corpus cavernosum penis, in which they rest in their natural state (*In Figs. 4 and 5, Model B conforms to above illustration from Sobotta, 1957; above figure is shown at two thirds the size of original drawn to natural size*)

body); and the crura (the legs). The crown is the part most familiar to us; indeed, along with its covering fold, it is usually thought of as the clitoris, as if it represented all of it. If the covering fold is drawn back, the crown is easily visible—a highly sensitive tip of flesh about the size of a small pea.

The corpus (or body), on the other hand, is not visible, but it can be felt with the fingertips just under the surface of the skin. It is usually about a quarter of an inch in diameter and somewhere less than an inch in length.

The crura (or legs), since they are internal structures, are not visible either; nor can they be easily felt. The two crura taper; in thickness, each one is somewhat less than the width of a little finger. In shape, they resemble an inverted "Y" or the Greek lambda λ. The shape in nature that most closely resembles it is the seed of a maple tree:

The idea of a male clitoris is startling to most people. Understandably, the visible parts of the male sexual organs are much more familiar than those inside the penis. For instance, just about everyone knows about the shaft of the penis, the foreskin, the glans, and the urethral opening through which both sexual fluids and urine are passed; but perhaps less well known is the body of tissue that surrounds the male urethra, called the spongiosum. And although everyone knows that the penis gets erect because it fills with blood, up to now very few have known about the part into which the blood flows, which is the male clitoris.

The following illustrations of life-size schematic models of the male and female clitoris make it clear that the male and female organs are very much alike; like the female, the male clitoris contains two crura, a corpus, and a crown (see Figures 4 and 5).

The two organs are also fairly close in size. A careful measure of the overall length shows five inches for the male and four inches for the female, making a 5:4 ratio. Since on the average men weigh approximately 160 pounds and women 128, one would expect such a difference to be reflected in the sizes

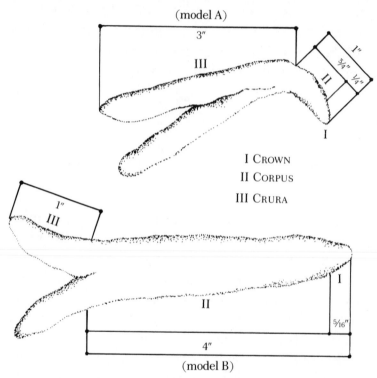

(model A)

I CROWN
II CORPUS
III CRURA

(model B)

FIG. 4 The Clitoris — Female (Model A) and Male (Model B) (*Model A is based on drawings of clitoral dissections by Regnier de Graaf shown in Fig. 7 and on Sobotta's illustration in Fig. 17; Model B is based on Sobotta's illustration shown in Fig. 3; above figure is shown at two thirds the size of original drawn to natural size*)

((20))

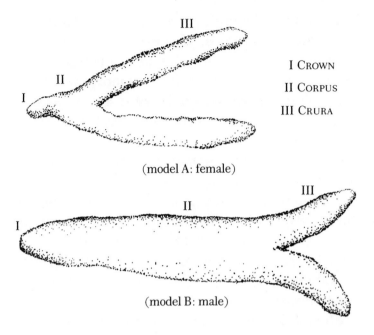

I Crown
II Corpus
III Crura

(model A: female)

(model B: male)

Fig. 5 The Clitoris — Female (Model A) and Male (Model B) (*Depicted in a perspective different from Fig. 4 to show greater degree of bifurcation in the female*)

of the parts that make up these weights, and the 5:4 ratio is exactly in line. On reflection, therefore, the traditional premise that the sexual parts of men and women are vastly different in size must be reconsidered.

The female clitoris has a *short* body that splits in two to form the long, separated legs, while the male clitoris has a *long* body that splits into two to form only very short, separated legs. But this difference is one of organization, not of substance. The female and male clitorises are composed of basically the same erectile substance.

There is only one basic difference between the

((*2 1*))

male and female Lowndes crowns: the female organ is an external structure, easily accessible to sight and to direct touch; the male is internal, but highly responsive nonetheless to indirect touch, or rather pressure. The implications of this for sexual arousal and the act of coitus is a topic to which I will return in a later chapter.

The Lowndes crowns theory is a two-part theory. The discovery of the male clitoris is the first part, but it raises a question: If the tip of the female clitoris is not the counterpart of the penile glans, is there another female part that *is*? There is indeed, and the part can be easily located and observed. If the inner folds (the labia minora) are spread apart, the opening of the urethra becomes clearly visible. The opening, called the meatus, is positioned immediately above the vaginal opening, which in most women is about three quarters of an inch beneath the Lowndes crown. The meatus is surrounded by a relatively prominent area shaped like an acorn, the back edge of which defines the opening of the vagina on its upper side. This same edge, in fact, defines both the beginning of the vagina and the end of the glans.

The edge itself has long been called the carina (the *carina urethralis vaginae*), but the prominent area as a whole has heretofore been left unnamed. This acorn-shaped prominence is the woman's glans. If it is recognized as such, the similarity between the woman's glans and the man's becomes obvious. Both have an overall acorn shape; both are perforated by the urethral opening; and the slightly raised female carina has its counterpart in the similar edge (the sulcus) of the man's glans (Figure 3). But what is more important to both men and women is that in

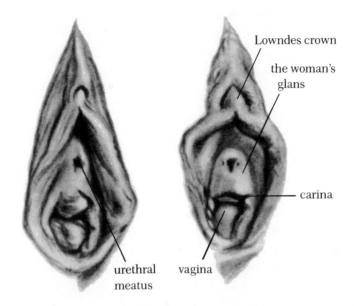

FIG. 6 Female Genitals (*Adapted from Robert Latou Dickinson*, Human Sex Anatomy, *Baltimore: Williams & Wilkins Company, 1949*)

both sexes the glans is richly endowed with nerve endings that make these parts exquisitely sensitive to touch.

In the description of the Lowndes crowns, we saw how the male parts tend to collect together, while the female's tend to split,* and this seems to be true overall in male and female genitalia.

The male glans closely covers the male Lowndes crown, whereas the woman's glans below and the exposed female Lowndes crown above are about three quarters of an inch apart.

*The external parts of women that are today called the vulva were in the Elizabethan period generally referred to as the great cleft—a term that had come down, with some embellishment, from the first-century language of Rufus.

((23))

Fig. 7 The Female Clitoris (*In Figs. 4 and 5, Model A conforms to this dissection drawn by Regnier de Graaf, 1672; this figure is shown at two thirds the size of original drawn to natural size*)

I shows the front of the clitoris

    A *clitoris*
    B *crura of the clitoris*
    C *glans of the clitoris*
    D *prepuce of the clitoris*
    E *nymphae*
    F *part of the periosteum by means of which the crura of the clitoris are connected to the lower part of the pubic bones*
    G *muscles of the clitoris*
    H *parts of the muscles which implant themselves in the bones of the ischium (or hip)*
    I *nerves*
    K *arteries* } *running to all parts of the pudendum*
    L *veins*

II shows the back of the clitoris

    A *clitoris*
    B *nymphae inverted*
    C *muscles running through the crura of the clitoris*
    D *fleshy fibers of the same muscles forming cavities of a kind*
    E *fleshy fibers of the sphincter, linked to the nervous substance of the clitoris*

III and IV show the clitoris dissected
in different ways

    a *clitoris*
    b *glans of clitoris with its nymphae*
    c *spongy substance of the clitoris divided through the middle by the septum*
    d *spongy substance of a crus divided through the middle by no septum*

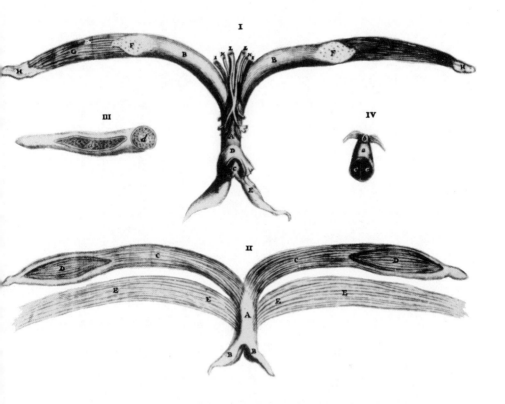

If you press a finger lightly against a woman's glans, it demonstrates a degree of mobility that allows it to be easily moved inside the vagina. The woman's glans is not a "fixed" organ; it has the potential for being moved around—not forward, but it can be pushed back. During coitus, the glans is pressed between the woman's pubic bone and her partner's penis; and penile thrusting makes the glans slide in and out of the vagina—creating a pleasurable sensation for the woman.

The facts about the female urethra and vagina in the chapters that follow round out what I believe to be compelling arguments for the plausibility of the new two-part theory. This book will discuss and rein-

Table 1 MALE AND FEMALE HOMOLOGUES

Galen's Theory		Modern Theory*		Lowndes Crowns Theory	
MALE	FEMALE	MALE	FEMALE	MALE	FEMALE
(1) Penis	Passageway of Vagina	(1) Penis	(1) Clitoris	(1) Clitoris	(1) Clitoris
		(a) *(Crown not yet identified)*	(a) *(Crown identified as "Glans"— see 2 below)*	(a) *Crown*	(a) *Crown*
		(b) Corpora cavernosa	(b) Corpora cavernosa	(b) *Corpus and Crura*	(b) *Corpus and Crura*
		(2) Glans Penis	(2) Glans Clitoridis	(2) Penile Glans	(2) Woman's Glans

*From the tabulation of Leslie B. Arey, *Developmental Anatomy: A Textbook and Laboratory Manual of Embryology*, (Philadelphia: W. B. Saunders Co., 1965; first published, 1924).

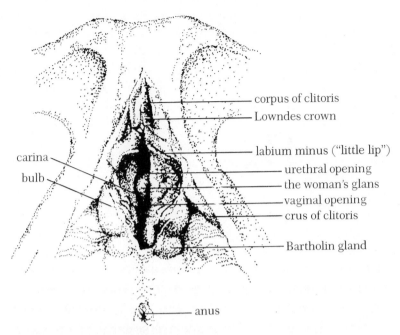

corpus of clitoris
Lowndes crown
labium minus ("little lip")
urethral opening
the woman's glans
vaginal opening
crus of clitoris
Bartholin gland
carina
bulb
anus

Fig. 8 Female Genitals (*Above figure is shown at two thirds the size of original drawn to natural size*)

terpret all the parts of the female genitals and related structures that function as sexual parts; it will also discuss a great deal about the male sexual parts, in order to describe in detail how the female and male counterparts are related.

CHAPTER 2

The Urethra

The new theory identifies the woman's glans and the glans of the penis as true counterparts. As we have seen, the woman's glans at the entrance to the vagina and the Lowndes crown visible on the vulval surface are separate from each other. In contrast, the man's glans, which is larger in circumference than the woman's, caps the male crown.

The glans in both sexes is the outermost part of the urethra. Until now, the female urethra has been thought of in Western culture only in connection with urination, and most women have not associated it with sex. But the naming and identification of the woman's glans raises the question: Is the female urethra a sexual organ?

The sexual function of the male urethra is, of course, officially recognized and immediately apparent—as are its urinary and reproductive functions—and every man is well aware of the urethra's sexual role.

If one traces the course of the male urethra from the opening at its surface to the bladder neck, three structures in addition to the glans can be identified:

1. the spongy portion around the passageway and the related bulbous structure,

2. the membranous portion,

3. the glandular portion,

Let us look more closely at each of these and compare them with the structures found in the female urethra.

1. The spongy portion that surrounds the urethral passageway, called the spongiosum, and the bulbous portion are so closely interrelated, it seems best to describe them in one combined section.

The prevailing theory contends that men have a

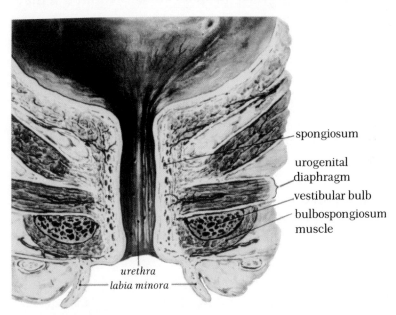

FIG. 9 Female Urogenital Structures: spongiosum and bulbs; membranous urethra (urogenital diaphragm)

spongiosum but women do not. In the female, the counterpart to the male spongiosum is supposedly limited to the vestibular bulbs, which are usually described as part of the clitoris, not the urethra. The female bulbs do, of course, have links with most of their adjacent parts, which include the clitoris. Certainly all these various parts (bulbs, clitoris, vagina, anus, and the urethra) are intimately interrelated. Indeed, among the points I want to emphasize is that of the simultaneous involvement of the clitoris, urethra, and vagina in sexual function. In order to explain how this works, I must first explain the basic organization of parts.

My new premise proposes to show that a female spongiosum does exist and that the vestibular bulbs should more logically be described as part of the organization of the female urethra.

The glans and the spongiosum represent one continuous structure. If there is a glans, there is a spongiosum (Figures 10, 11). A comparison of the female and male urethras in cross-section provides even clearer evidence of the fact that similar spongy portions exist in both sexes (Figures 12 and 13). In the female urethra, between the thin lining of the passageway and the surrounding layers of muscle, there is a layer of spongy, erectile substance. According to my theory, this spongy portion is the female spongi-

FIG. 10 Male Urogenital Structures: glans; spongiosum and bulbs; membranous urethra (urogenital diaphragm); prostate

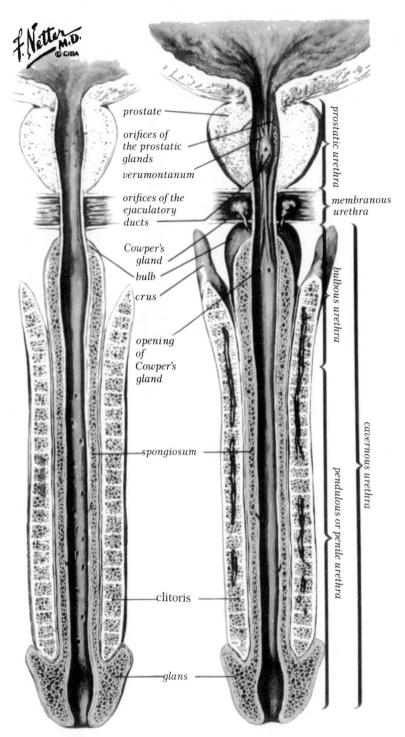

prostate

orifices of
the prostatic
glands

verumontanum

prostatic urethra

orifices of the
ejaculatory
ducts

membranous
urethra

Cowper's
gland

bulb

crus

opening
of
Cowper's
gland

bulbous urethra

spongiosum

cavernous urethra

pendulous or penile urethra

clitoris

glans

roof

floor

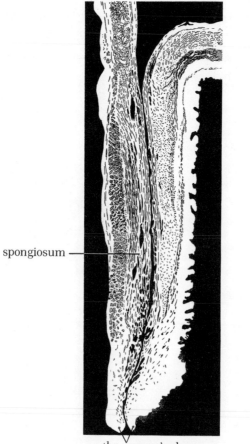
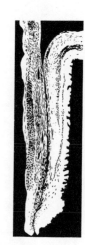

spongiosum ——

the woman's glans

FIG. 11 Adult Female Urethra — Mid-sagittal Section. Inset shows approximate natural length of urethra (*Adapted from A. B. Huisman,* Contributions to Gynecology and Obstetrics, *Vol. 10, 1983*)

osum—the counterpart of the corresponding spongy portion in the male urethra.

In the male, the spongiosum is about five inches long and thinnest at its tip where it merges with the glans; it widens as it approaches the root of the penis inside the body and bulges considerably at its termination point, where it forms a pear-shaped bulb. Except for the bulb, the spongiosum is much thinner than the corpus (the body) of the male clitoris (Figure 16).

The bulb does not divide into two halves, but the suggestion of such a division exists in the form of a shallow groove on the surface (the sulcus bulbi). The bulb itself is situated between the crura of the clitoris so that the passageway courses above the bulb, not through it. The fullest expansion of the bulbous portion (about an inch) pushes toward the anus.

2. The female spongiosum completely surrounds the passageway and extends for about an inch and a half from the glans along the length of the urethra to the bladder neck. In thickness, it is fairly constant—about a half inch (1 to 1.5 cm)—but it thins somewhat near the glans (outside the body) and broadens a lit-

(a) spongiosum

(b) passageway

(c) muscle coat (smooth)

(d) muscle coat (striated)

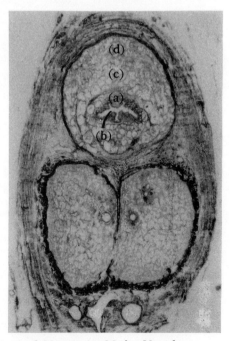

FIG. 12 Cross Section of Neonate Male Urethra (*Adapted from J.A.G. Rhodin*, Histology: A Text and Atlas, *1974*)

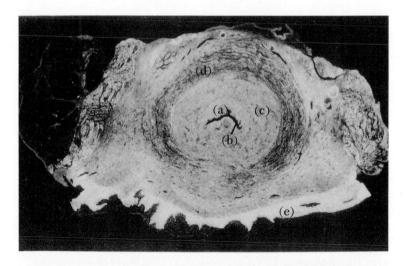

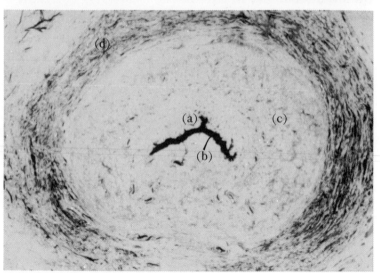

FIG. 13 Cross Section and Detail Enlargement of Neonate Female Urethra *(Adapted from A. B. Huisman, Contributions to Gynecology and Obstetrics, Vol. 10, 1983)*

(a) spongiosum   (c) muscle coat (smooth)
(b) passageway   (d) muscle coat (striated)
         (e) ceiling of vagina

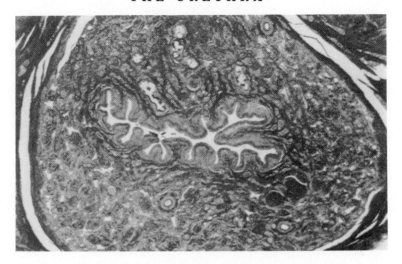

FIG. 14 Cross Section Through Spongy Portion of Adult Male Urethra *(From F. Hammersen and J. Sobotta, Histology, 1980)*

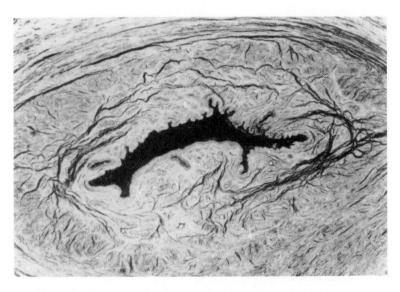

FIG. 15 Cross Section Through Spongy Portion of Adult Female Urethra *(Adapted from A. B. Huisman, Contri-butions to Gynecology and Obstetrics, Vol. 10, 1983)*

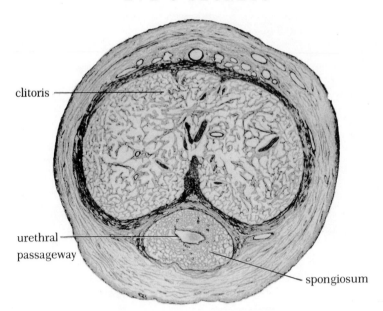

clitoris

urethral passageway

spongiosum

FIG. 16 Male Spongiosum in Relation to Male Clitoris (*Adapted from A. Maximow and W. Bloom*, A Textbook of Histology, *1957*)

tle as it approaches the pelvic area behind the pubic bone (inside the body).

3. *The same kind of erectile tissue found in the male and female spongiosum can be found in the male bulb and in the female vestibular bulbs.* These bulbous erectile tissues clearly relate to the urethral structure. Therefore, it seems only logical—and, in fact, much more illuminating in terms of sexual function—to associate the female bulbs primarily with the urethra rather than with the clitoris.

The female bulbs take the overall form of a highly arched crescent with their fullness at the bottom, just above each Bartholin gland on each side of the vagina. They are located between the vaginal lining and the left and right legs of the clitoris (Figure 17). The bulbs taper upward and connect in a narrow

band (the commissure) at the peak of the arch, between the urethra and the Lowndes crown. In this
position, the bulbous structure at its peak embraces
the urethra but is separate from the passageway. As
noted, the male bulb, like that of its female counterpart, also is separate from the urethral passageway.
The bulbous structures differ in the sexes in that the
male has one bulb, the female two.

4. Each vestibular bulb is about an inch and a
half long, a half-inch wide, and about three eighths
of an inch thick; and each is covered by the bulbo-
spongiosum muscle (Figure 17). The male bulb has a
similar covering muscle, but the female's is much

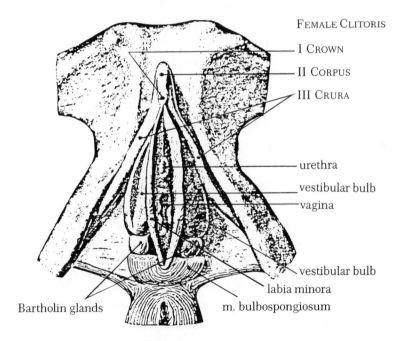

FEMALE CLITORIS
I CROWN
II CORPUS
III CRURA

urethra
vestibular bulb
vagina

vestibular bulb
labia minora
m. bulbospongiosum

Bartholin glands

FIG. 17 Erectile Bodies of the Female Genitals (*In Figs.
4 and 5, Model A is based on above illustration adapted
from Sobotta, 1957; above figure is shown at two thirds
the size of original drawn to natural size*)

more extensive—about three inches overall. Up to now, the focus of attention in medical books has been on the muscle's role in causing the female bulbs to swell, an action that makes the vaginal opening smaller; hence the traditional preference for referring to this musculature in the female not as the bulbo-spongiosum but rather as the "vaginal sphincter." I will discuss later the pleasurable sensations a woman is able to receive as well as give as a result of the bulbo-spongiosum's action.

The above four points and accompanying illustrations adapted from the work of a number of scientists provide evidence in support of my premise that the female spongiosum, together with the vestibular bulbs, corresponds to the male spongiosum and bulb.

Any tissue that has the capacity to fill with blood and become swollen is called erectile tissue. But the word "erection," as we all know, carries a different connotation. English-speaking people almost automatically identify the word "erection" with the male body. Some of us would perhaps have to think twice if we came across a reference to "female erection," although, in one sense, the term is not incorrect. When either men or women are sexually excited, their urethral and clitoral structures swell. When swollen, the spongy portions in both sexes are still relatively soft compared to the clitoris. The same is true for the bulbs, particularly for the female bulbs. The vestibular bulbs are made up of many nets of veins, which upon sexual stimulation cause the bulbs to swell and become pillowy soft. In contrast the clitoral structures in both sexes, firmer to begin with, become even firmer, which is, of course, much more noticeable in the male than in the female. In this sense of "erectile," then, it is possible to say that both sexes have erections.

"Erection," however, also implies an upward motion. When a man's penis is stimulated and builds from the pendulous to the erect position, the glans can describe an arc in the air in full erection to an upper anatomical limit of 120 degrees, according to Dickinson, who notes that 110 degrees agrees best with anatomical studies of the erect phallus with man standing.* Nothing in the female sexual anatomy can be said to go "up" in quite the same way the penis does. Therefore, those who wonder about the appropriateness of using the term "erection" in relation to the female have some justification. Nevertheless female erection is a reality.

According to the old theory of homologues, the clitoris was the counterpart of the penis, and the vestibular bulbs, though listed as part of the clitoris, were accepted as the counterpart of the male spongy portion (see Appendix D—Corpus Cavernosum Urethrae). I have presented existing scientific evidence of a female spongy portion around the urethra and reasons why both this structure and the two vestibular bulbs should now more logically be accepted as counterparts of the male spongy portion and its one bulb. The comparative lengths of these counterparts—five inches in the male and four and a half inches in the female (spongiosum, one and a half inches; bulbs, three inches)—come very close to achieving the same 5:4 ratio found between the male and female clitorises. The main difference between the two is the difference in the organization of the

*Robert Latou Dickinson, *Human Sex Anatomy*, 2nd ed. (Baltimore: Williams & Wilkins Company, 1949), Figure 112.

structures—the male pattern tending toward the unification of parts and the female's toward bifurcation, as in the cases of the clitoris and the glans.

Between the spongy and glandular portions of the urethra, a thin, shelflike layer of tissue stretches across the area of the pubic arch. This is called the urogenital diaphragm. It exists in both sexes, and is located at the level of the urethra directly behind the

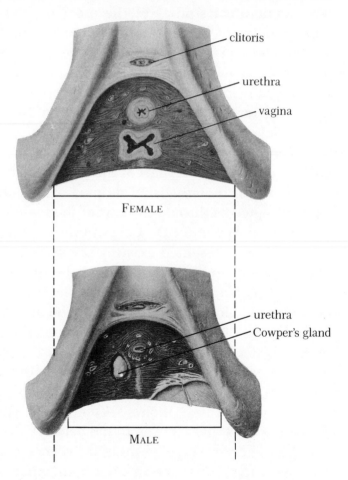

FIG. 18 The Urogenital Diaphragm (*Adapted from J. Sobotta,* Atlas of Descriptive Human Anatomy, *1957*)

pubic bone (Figure 18). Before the urethral passageway can reach the body surface, it has to perforate
the diaphragm. In women, the vagina also perforates
it. Since the pubic arch is wider in women, the diaphragm is accordingly wider (Figure 18). In men, the
diaphragm measures less than three quarters of an
inch (about 18 mm) from bottom to top; in women, the
part is not quite that high.

Despite the above known facts, the prevailing
embryological theory contends that women do not
have a membranous urethra, recognizing instead
only the middle part of the vestibule as the homologue of the membranous urethra,* a portion attributed in the scientific literature to the male alone.
It seems arbitrary—if not downright illogical—to
claim that a section of the urethra that is similarly
located and surrounded by a structurally similar diaphragm in both sexes exists only in the male and not
in the female. Traditionally, names for sections of
the urethra itself have been based on the specific
types of structures through which the urethra passes
at various points. If these surrounding structures are
the same in both sexes, as in this instance, and if the
nomenclature for the male and female urethras is to
be consistent, it would only make sense to use the
same term for both sexes, as I propose to do.

In both sexes, the membranous urethra is surrounded by a similar sphincter muscle (the sphincter
membranaceae urethra). This section, compared to
the portions below and above it, has the least degree
of distensibility, the passageway here being more

---

*The premise is that the male membranous urethra and the
female vestibule are both derived from the same pelvic portion
of the urogenital sinus in the embryo.

((*41*))

"fixed" in position by the surrounding diaphragm and sphincter muscle. The female membranous urethra is relatively more distensible than the male,* and contains spongy tissue, which the male does not.

The glandular portion of the urethra, called the prostate in the male, produces a sexual fluid. This makes it of central importance in any consideration of sexual function; hence it is of equal importance to the idea of sexual symmetries between the sexes. Men and women are generally aware of the male prostate and its fluid, but not many are aware that similar glands exist in women. The existence of a female prostate and female ejaculation was accepted without question in earlier times. In recent years, however, the idea has often been denied. The search for a resolution of this controversy has led to a new theory that provides some answers about female sexual fluids, the true source of which has for so long remained a mystery. The theory is predicated on evidence of the existence of prostatic glands in women. This evidence, which has existed in the scientific literature for centuries, is discussed next in Chapter 3 in the context of the female sexual secretions. Although these fluid-producing glandular structures are found in both men and women, a comparison of the two reveals certain differences in anatomical form, size, and number of ducts. Also here again, in terms of organization, one sees the same pattern of male fusion/female diffusion.

In the male, the prostate consists of a group of

*So is the female passageway overall, which—though shorter—can be dilated to a much wider aperture, should the need arise in clinical procedures.

POSTERIOR VIEW

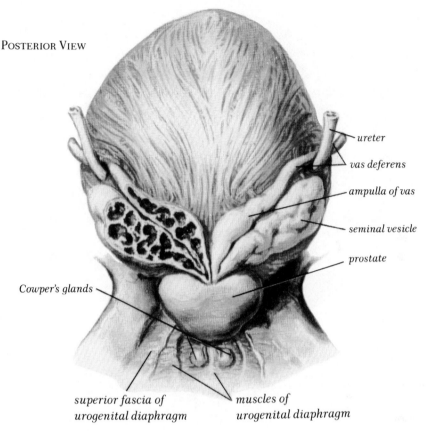

ureter

vas deferens

ampulla of vas

seminal vesicle

prostate

Cowper's glands

superior fascia of
urogenital diaphragm

muscles of
urogenital diaphragm

FIG. 19 The Urinary Bladder of a Man, Showing Posterior View of the Prostate Gland

glands collected into an organ the shape and size of a chestnut about one inch long (Figure 19). As many as ten to twenty prostatic ducts open onto the urethra in one small concentrated area called the verumontanum (Figures 10, 19). Here sperm mixes with the fluid from the prostate and other male fluids before

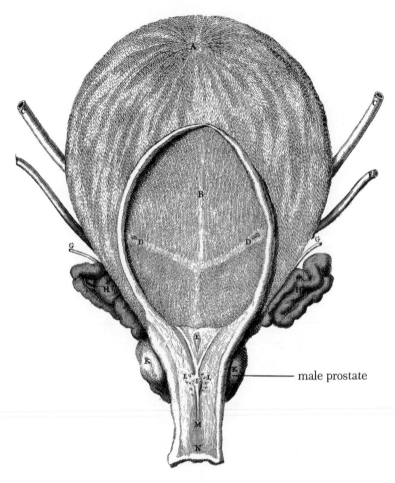

male prostate

FIG. 20 The Urinary Bladder of a Man, Showing the Prostate Gland (*Above figure is shown at two thirds the size of original drawn to natural size by Regnier de Graaf, 1668*)

A *part of the urinary bladder to which the urachus was attached*
B *urinary bladder opened at the front*
C *ureters*
D *exits of the ureters into the bladder*
E *neck of the bladder*
F *parts of the vasa deferentia cut*

G *vessels running to the seminal vesicles*

H *seminal vesicles inflated*

I *small piece of flesh with the two holes through which
semen from the testicles, or rather the seminal vesicles,
discharges into the urethra*

K *prostate gland divided at the front*

L *mouths of the ducts of the prostate gland opening at the
sides of the small piece of flesh and only visible at certain
points except when the ducts are inflated*

M *beak of the small piece of flesh, which resembles
a rooster's head*

N *urethra opened at the top*

being ejaculated.* Lengthwise, the prostate extends from the diaphragm upward to the bladder neck, and since the part is situated on the rear wall of the urethra, it bulges against the rectum.

In the female, the prostatic glands are dispersed along the floor of the urethra. Their distribution lengthwise is highly variable, a variability that has been attributed to a number of possible factors, including parity (the fact of having borne offspring), hormonal makeup, and age. In adult women, these structures are found in greater abundance toward the bladder end of the urethra; in the newborn, they are more likely to exist at the opposite end, closer to the urethral opening. Whatever the age of the female, however, these glandular structures are con-

---

*The path of the sperm through the male passages has been traced. The sperm comes from the testicles via tubes (the vas deferens); these tubes join other structures called the seminal vesicles (see Figure 10), where they form a common ejaculatory duct. The male ejaculate, or seminal fluid, is a mixture of sperm from the testes and fluids from the so-called accessory glands— that is, principally from the prostate and the seminal vesicles, and a small amount from the Cowper's glands (also called the bulbourethral glands).

sistently located on the floor of the urethra, thus creating a bulge that pushes into the vagina.

The urethra and the vagina are inseparable from each other and, in this area, form a common "wall." Even though this area is usually referred to in this way, the urethra and the vagina are not side by side, as the word "wall" suggests; rather, the "floor" of the urethra is the "ceiling" of the vagina. Along the length of this section of the vagina are embedded the female prostatic glands. The adult female urethra and prostatic glands may contain as many as thirty-one ducts (Figure 21). The glands extend for a variable length—usually less than an inch,

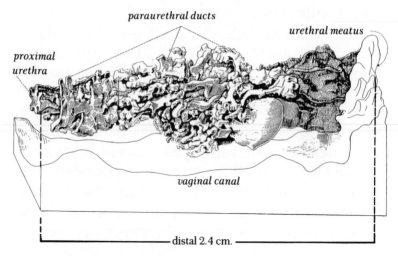

FIG. 21 The Female Prostatic Glands: drawing of a wax model of an adult human female urethra and surrounding prostatic glands, representing the distal 2.4 cm. of a total length of 2.8 cm., containing 31 ducts; tissues obtained at necropsy of a twenty-year-old virgin. (*Adapted from J. W. Huffman,* American Journal of Obstetrics and Gynecology, *Vol. 55 (1): 86–101, 1948*)

FIG. 22 The Female Prostatic Glands, Shown Closer to
Natural Size (with contour of bulge into ceiling of vagina
outlined) (*Adapted from J. W. Huffman, 1948*)

but in some cases almost two inches—beyond which
point the vagina usually smooths out to a more
velvety texture. When sexually stimulated, the area
may swell in diameter.

In men, the swelling of prostatic tissue, unlike
the conspicuous swelling of penile tissue, is hidden.
In women, it is possible to observe the swelling of the
urethral structure and prostatic glands in the roof of
the vagina; in the sexual setting, however, this female swelling is more easily discerned by feel. A gentle, slow stroking of a finger from side to side (rather
than an in-and-out motion) just inside the top of the
vaginal opening reveals the bulge this structure creates.

A physician, Dr. S. Richard Muellner, contends
that the human female's urethra has been needlessly
made into "a mystery wrapped in an enigma."* His
interest was the treatment for disorders of the female
urethra; mine is its anatomy and function, but I
agree—there is no need for this part of the female
anatomy to continue to be a mystery. With the knowl-

*S. Richard Muellner, "The Anatomics of the Female Ure-
thra: A Critical Review," *Obstetrics and Gynecology* 14:4, October 1959, p. 434.

edge we now have about the existence of the woman's glans, the spongiosum, and the prostatic glands, it can no longer remain a secret that the female urethra is a sexual organ.

CHAPTER 3

The Female Fluids

1. The "Fecund Fluids"

One of the fundamental principles around which ideas about female fluids were formulated was the early philosophical belief in a *liquor vitae* as the primary vehicle of life.

Hippocrates (460–377 B.C.), who helped to free medicine from superstition and speculation, advocated a "two semen" theory of generation predicated on the belief that both the male and female sexual fluids contributed to conception.* In his seventeenth-century treatise on women, Regnier de Graaf mentions that those who followed Hippocrates argued that "women are beset by nocturnal pollutions [wet dreams] just as much as men and both in widows and maidens who suffer from hysterical fits, thick and copious quantities of semen pour from the genital parts if these are tickled."†

*Hippocrates, *De genitura,* chap. 6 (7.478), and *De Diaeta,* I.27 (6.500). See Regnier de Graaf, *New Treatise Concerning the Generative Organs of Women,* 1672, p. 136.

†Regnier de Graaf, in H. D. Jocelyn and B. P. Setchell, trans., *Journal of Reproduction and Fertility, op. cit.,* p. 137.

Pythagorus (580–495 B.C.) believed that the generative fluid of the female was the foam of pure blood and that it trickled from the brain. Democritos (450 B.C.) thought that the fluid was derived from all parts of the body, which is in a sense not incorrect. Parmenides (450 B.C.) held that the good constitution of infants depended on the union of a proper mixture of male and female genital fluid. Diogenes (c. 430 B.C.) considered the generative fluid of the female an "air" which emanated from the spermatic veins (the veins leading to the reproductive organs) during coitus.

Aristotle (384–322 B.C.), on the other hand, contended that the power of generation resided exclusively in the "seminal liquor" of the male. According to this idea, men alone controlled the magical force of conception; it was the father—not the mother—who was the true parent of the newborn. In the Aristotelian view, man controlled the form of new life; women only provided the "matter." As a result, the status of women suffered. Those who supported this view believed that the female fluid served only to nourish the fetus; that the mother was a nutritive nurse to the offspring, in much the same way that the earth is to seed.

Galen (130–200) opposed Aristotle's view, and supported the earlier belief of Hippocrates that both men and women produce seed. In elaborating upon the description of the female fluids in his writings, Galen made a distinction between the fluids from the female prostate and those from other parts:

> Since the female is more frigid than the male, the fluid in her prostate is unconcocted and thin. This contributes nothing to the generation of off-

spring.* Properly, then, it is poured outside when it has done its service. . . . This liquid not only stimulates to the sexual act but also is able to give pleasure and moisten the passageway as it escapes. It manifestly flows from women as they experience the greatest pleasure in coitus, when it is perceptibly shed upon the male pudendum; indeed, such an outflow seems to give a certain pleasure even to eunuchs. Thus you could not want a clearer proof than this.†

In using the word "frigid," Galen does not mean to connote sexual apathy as the modern sense of the word suggests; rather, he is actually referring to the temperature of the human organs. His ideas on the subject are clearly influenced by the "heat" thesis of Empedocles, who, writing around the year 460 B.C., had proposed that all living matter was made up of the hot and cold elements found in nature. According to Empedocles, the "hot" elements, such as air and fire, were associated with the male, and the "cold," such as earth and water, with the female. Thus Galen evidently presumed it was correct to impute relative "coldness" to the female, in contrast to the superior quality of relative "hotness" credited to the male.

The man is more perfect than the woman, and the reason for his perfection is his excess heat, for heat is Nature's primary instrument. Hence in those animals that have less of it, her workman-

*Galen, *On the Usefulness of the Parts (De usu partium)*, Book 14.11. The first portion of the quote (*) tr. by the author; the second portion (†) tr. by Margaret Tallmade May, *op. cit.*, p. 645. May notes that some scholars consider this passage highly suspect because of its contents and that, in fact, it does not appear in all translations.

ship is necessarily more imperfect, and so it is no wonder that the female is less perfect than the male by as much as she is colder than he.*

In this concept of the physiology of body fluids, Galen attributed great importance to the role of heat. He believed that as the body becomes hotter, the increased heat factor serves to drain fluid from muscle tissues, causing the muscles to get dry and to contract. The heat and the muscle contractions, in turn, cause the nerves to shorten "like a rope in the sun," thereby bringing about the interaction of muscle and nerve necessary for function.

Though great controversies existed as to which theory of generation was the correct one, there was agreement about one thing—the mystery was linked to the sexual fluids.

Historically, goddesses of nature were often associated with the waters of the earth and bodily fluids, the sources of all life. The Egyptian goddess Ishtar, for example, was goddess of the seas and tides and women's menstrual fluids. From Ishtar evolved the Greek goddess Aphrodite, later to become the Latin Venus, born of the waters of the earth, and the medieval Mary, Queen of Nature, whose name is derived from the Latin *mare,* meaning "sea." In *The Virgin,* Geoffrey Ashe refers to Mary as the "All Holy Aphrodite."

In India, the Absolute is believed to be female, and the mother goddess is worshipped under a number of different names, not only as the maternal provider and nourisher but also as sex goddess. Uma, the wife of Siva; Kali, the terrifying, black earth mother;

*Margaret Tallmadge May, *op. cit.,* p. 630.

and Lakshmi, Vishnu's wife, are but a few of the names she has, many of which are not to be found in books but are part of the vocabulary of Indian villagers, who turn to these protectresses of fertility as they have done for at least five thousand years.

From about the fourth century B.C., one of the female goddesses worshipped by the Hebrews was Asherah of the Sea, who was believed to help women become more fertile and to ease childbirth. In *The Hebrew Goddess,* Raphael Patai mentions that the name of Asherah was often used interchangeably with Astarte, indicating a lack of clear distinction between the functions and personalities of these two goddesses that is found in the Bible and persists among scholars. "Asherah was a motherly goddess and as such she, together with her daughter Anath, served as the wetnurse of the gods," Patai informs us.* On the other hand, Astarte, the Greek name for a warrior goddess, was also the goddess of sexual love and fertility. She is thought to be the goddess for whom Hebrew women made cakes and burned incense as part of fertility rituals. An ivory plaque believed to be a representation of Astarte was found in Mesopotamia about the eighth century B.C. It depicts her, like her temple prostitutes, gazing from her window for all eternity to lure men. Patai also tells us about Matronit, who, like a true goddess, played the double role of spouse and mother, and that "to this day, in every Jewish temple or synagogue she is welcomed in the Friday evening prayers with the words 'Come, O bride!' " And we must not overlook Lilith, Adam's first wife, who left him and went on eventu-

*Raphael Patai, *The Hebrew Goddess* (New York: Avon Books, 1978), p. 20.

ally to become the consort of God himself.

According to the anthropologist Bronislaw Malinowski, early man had no awareness of the connection between the sexual act and birth, and for this reason the mystery of birth was first identified solely with the female.* And because men had no inkling of their own contribution to conception, they viewed both as the result of female magic. Women's sexual parts, from which life emerges, held prehistoric man in fear and awe. In bas-reliefs, cave paintings, figurines, and slabs, there are depictions of the female body and symbols of the female genitals believed to be symbols of fertility and the earliest objects of men's worship (Figures 23, 24).

If women were worshipped because men believed that the female of the species conceived children by herself, how did the rule of men come about? As Evelyne Sullerot concludes in *Woman, Society and Change,* the link that would explain how the rule of men succeeded that of women has always been missing.† But a possible explanation of the shift comes down to us through legend. As Joseph Campbell explains in his study of primitive mythology, *The Masks of God: Primitive Mythology,* the legend of the Ona of Tierra del Fuego tells of a massacre that ended the age of female magic. Because men felt tyrannized by women who were more powerful in their society, they conspired to massacre all females, sparing only the younger girls to be raised as their future wives. According to E. Lucas Bridges, who is

*Bronislaw Malinowski, *Sexual Life of Savages* (London: Routledge & Sons, 1929).

†Evelyne Sullerot, *Woman, Society and Change,* trans. by Margaret Scotford Archer (New York: McGraw-Hill, 1971).

Fig. 23 The Venus of Willendorf (*Naturhistorisches Museum, Vienna*)

cited by Campbell, "This legend of leadership being wrested from the women, either by force or coercion, is too widely spread throughout the world to be lightly ignored."* In *Memory of Fire: Genesis,* Eduard Galeano tells the story of the same legend as recorded by contemporary anthropologists:

*Passage from E. Lucas Bridges, *The Uttermost Parts of the Earth* (New York: E. P. Dutton, 1948), p. 262, cited in Joseph Campbell, *The Masks of God: Primitive Mythology* (New York: The Viking Press, 1974), p. 314.

FIG. 24 Engraved Vulvae from La Ferrassie, Dordogne, France, Aurignacian Rock (*Musée de Eyzies*)

In remote times women sat in the bow of the canoe and men in the stern. It was the women who hunted and fished. They left the villages and returned when they could or wanted. The men built the huts, prepared the meals, kept the fires burning against the cold, minded the children, and tanned skins for clothes.

Such was the life for the Ona and Yagan Indians in Tierra del Fuego, until one day the men killed all the women and put on the masks that the women had invented to scare them.

Only newly born girls were spared extermination. While they grew up, the murderers kept repeating to them that serving men was their destiny. They believed it. Their daughters believed it, too, likewise the daughters of their daughters.*

*Eduard Galeano, *Memory of Fire: Genesis,* trans. by Cedric Belfrage (New York: Pantheon Books, 1985), p. 36.

But this is myth and legend; we don't really know.

In Western religions, God is male, and authority rests with men; but birth has always been viewed as a tangible evidence of divine power, to be controlled by divine law. The very human matter of bodily fluids and sexual practices that controlled their release or the withholding of these fluids was a matter of grave religious concern in both the Jewish and the early Christian faiths. Thus, the influences that shaped the ideas of Western medicine concerning female sexual fluids can be traced in the Judaic/ Christian doctrinal documents.

In the Babylonian Talmud, compiled around A.D. 500, one can find a whole tractate devoted to the subject of menstrual and other female fluids.* It is called the *Niddah,* and deals with the uncleanness of the "menstruant" as set forth in the Old Testament of the Bible:

> And if a woman have an issue, and her issue in her flesh be blood, she shall be put apart seven days; and whosoever toucheth her shall be unclean until the even *(Leviticus 15:19).*

> Also thou shall not approach unto a woman to uncover her nakedness, as long as she is put apart for her uncleanness *(Leviticus 18:19).*

> And if a man shall lie with a woman having her sickness, and shall uncover her nakedness, he hath discovered her fountain, and she hath uncovered the fountain of her blood; and both of them shall be cut off from among their people *(Leviticus 20:18).*

*In the early centuries of the first millennium A.D., a rich collection of rabbinical texts on laws was compiled, which cla-

The "Mishnah," the first code of Rabbinic law, compiled by Rabbi Jehuda Hanasi in Palestine around A.D. 200, goes into precise ritualistic regulations that govern the purification of the menstruating woman (*Niddah,* 14a).

In the minutely detailed writings of the *Niddah,* a reference is also made to a "white" and a "red" female discharge. The red obviously refers to menstrual blood. The white, a discharge that "causes no uncleanliness in a woman," is described as resembling semen (*Niddah,* 78a). We can reasonably presume this to be the female prostatic fluid (mixed with other genital fluids of the female ejaculate).

In the Jewish faith, male fluids also were subject to religious law. In Leviticus, the section on the "cleansing of issues" includes the male seminal fluid as well. According to Biblical law, seminal fluid from the male had a polluting effect on both the individual male and any woman or object it touched or that touched the man:

> And if any man's seed of copulation go out from him, then he shall wash all his flesh in water, and be unclean until the even. And every garment, and every skin, whereon is the seed of copulation, shall be washed with water, and be unclean until the even. The woman also with whom man shall lie with seed of copulation, they shall both bathe themselves in water, and be unclean until the even. [Leviticus 15:16–18]

---

rified, interpreted, and expanded upon the legendary laws of the prophets. The Hebrew prophets of the Old Testament are thought to have lived in the period from the ninth to the sixth centuries B.C.

Since the basic concern of rabbinical law was to prevent any wastage of the fluids of generation, there were laws pertaining to frequency of coitus and sexual practices considered to be a sinful waste of the fluids. Rabbis established a "love tariff" whereby a peasant was allowed to have sexual intercourse with his wife once a week; a tradesman once a month; a sailor twice a year; and a man of letters once in two years.*

In the *Midrash Rabbah,* the Great Flood is described as a punishment for the sin of male coitus interruptus—the tabooed practice described elsewhere as the act whereby men "poured out their semen upon trees and stones." The practice was considered to be such an outrageous abuse of the natural order that the Lord punished his people by reversing the natural order of the waters of the earth. Since in the natural order the rains fall and the seas rise, the Lord made the seas rise and after that "the windows of heaven were opened" and the rain descended (*Midrash Rabbah,* p. 255; Genesis [Noab], 32:7).

In *Nederim* (20a), there is a reference to an unnatural act euphemistically described as a couple "overturning their table"—that is, the act of coitus with the woman on top. This forbidden, unnatural act can be traced in Hebrew myth back to the story of Lilith (or Lilas). In his book on tabooed subjects privately printed in London in 1875, from which we have already quoted, John Davenport mentions that many rabbis assert that "in the beginning God created two women, one of whom was named Lilas and the other Eve; the first being created simultane-

*John Davenport, *Curiositates Eroticae Physiologicae: or, Tabooed Subjects Freely Treated* (London, 1875).

ously with Adam, and, like him, of the dust of the ground, while the other was fashioned from one of his ribs." Davenport states that he is quoting from "the celebrated Buxtorf" who wrote about the history of the first wife of Adam, how she, having destroyed him, divorced herself from him and endeavored to destroy their son as soon as he was born.

Robert Graves and Raphael Patai also write about the fact that in the Hebrew *Midrashim** Lilith, Eve's predecessor, is included in the Creation myth in Genesis:

> Adam and Lileth never found peace together; when he wished to lie with her, she took offence at the recumbent posture he demanded. "Why must I lie beneath you?" she asked. "I also was made from dust, and am therefore your equal." Because Adam tried to compel her obedience by force, Lileth, in a rage, uttered the magic name of God, rose into the air and left him.†

Graves and Patai go on to explain:

> It is characteristic of civilizations where women are treated as chattels that they must adopt the recumbent posture during intercourse, which Lileth refused. That Greek witches who worshipped Hecate favored the superior posture, we know from Apuleius; and it occurs in early Sumerian representations of the sexual act, though not in the Hittite. Malinowski writes that

*Earlier, these authors had pointed out that although Lilith has been included in this rabbinic literature, she has been wholly exorcised from Scripture. The *Midrashim* (plural of *Midrash*) were written and compiled from A.D. 100 to about 1100.

†Robert Graves and Raphael Patai, *Hebrew Myths: The Book of Genesis* (Garden City, N.Y.: Doubleday & Company, 1964), p. 65.

Melanesian girls ridicule what they call "the mis-
sionary position," which demands that they
should lie passive and recumbent.*

At the root of the "pollution" taboos is the fundamental religious concern of the rabbis to foster and
protect the procreative process of their people. The
same concern is at the root of Christian doctrine. The
teachings of the New Testament do not, however,
present the same kind of systematic code of controls
over sexual practices as is found in the Old Testament, and over the centuries the Catholic Church has
come to rely more on verbal pastoral guidance than
on the written catechisms of the early Christians or
the explicit confessional manuals of the Middle
Ages, which were used by some priests well into the
seventeenth century. But it has a Code of Canon Law
and from time to time issues papal encyclicals that,
while not considered to be infallible, serve as clear
statements of the Church's position on important issues, including those that relate to marriage and
marital acts.

In the Catholic faith, the primary end of matrimony is procreation (*Canon*, 1013). In the encyclical
letter of Pope Paul VI, the *Humanae Vitae,* the Pope
reminded his people that any direct interruption of
the generative process once begun is condemned by
the Church. "Similarly excluded is any action, which
either before, at the moment of, or after sexual intercourse, is specifically intended to prevent procreation—whether as an end or as a means."†

*Graves and Patai, *op. cit.,* pp. 68–69.
†Pope Paul VI, Encyclical on Human Life *(Humanae Vitae),*
1968.

From medieval times to the present, one of the marital acts excluded by the Church is *amplexus reservatus,* a contraceptive method whereby the ejaculation of fluids is purposely withheld by both the man and the woman. Condemned by medieval confessors, the practice was cited again as objectionable in a notice dated June 30, 1952, from the Holy Office, which appeared in the *Acta Apostolicae Sedis** on the express mandate of Pope Pius XII. As translated in *The Irish Ecclesiastical Record,* the notice states:

> . . . the Apostolic See is gravely concerned to note that a number of present-day writers have, in an unreserved and shamelessly detailed manner, dealt with matters relating to conjugal life and that a few of these writers have described, praised and recommended the act known as *amplexus reservatus.* Consequently the Holy Office in fulfillment of its important duty of safeguarding the sanctity of marriage and the salvation of souls, gravely warns these writers that they must desist from this manner of writing and exposition. The Holy Office earnestly exhorts bishops to exercise strict vigilance in this matter and to appoint suitable remedies. The final paragraph of the *Monitum* is addressed to priests. In their work of the care of souls and the direction of consciences they should never, either spontaneously

*AAS is the monthly journal of the Holy See named by Canon Law as the authoritative publication of the Catholic Church to keep members informed of official actions. All decrees and decisions of the Roman Rota printed in the *AAS* are officially promulgated and become effective three months from the date of their promulgation.

or in reply to a question, presume so to speak of the *amplexus reservatus* as if there were no objection to it from the standpoint of Christian law.*

The significance of this notice to the history of female sexual fluids is that it provides a record of the centuries-long recognition of the fact that women experience an ejaculation of fluids comparable to that of the male. This almost certainly dates back to the knowledge provided by Galen about the female prostatic fluid (see page 50). According to John T. Noonan, theologians believed that "there is a parallel between male ejaculation and pleasure and female ejaculation and pleasure."†

Steven Ozment, professor of history at Harvard, also mentions that "such contraceptive methods as *amplexus reservatus,* the willed suppression of semination on the part of *both* sexes (dry orgasm), and *coitus interruptus,* the diversion of male semen from the womb, were among the sexual practices condemned by confessors."‡

Still thinking of these female fluids as the "fecund" (or fertile) fluids, the Church forbids women *not* to ejaculate. The world of science, on the other hand—perhaps because it was unduly influenced by the nineteenth-century ideal of female sexlessness—came to deny that women *could* ejaculate, a highly ironic turn of events.

*The Irish Ecclesiastical Record, 79: 57–60, January 1953.
†John T. Noonan, Jr., *Contraception: A History of Its Treatment by the Catholic Theologians and Canonists* (Cambridge, Mass.: The Belknap Press, Harvard University Press, 1965), p. 337.
‡Steven Ozment, *When Fathers Ruled: Family Life in Reformation Europe* (Cambridge, Mass.: Harvard University Press, 1983), p. 216.

2. *The Sexual Secretions*

In past centuries, the ejaculation of female fluids during sexual stimulation was accepted by men and women as a natural part of sex, the phenomenon being very much a part of folk knowledge in our own and other cultures and an established piece of medical knowledge. Despite this, most twentieth-century physicians have denied the existence of female ejaculation. No one, of course, denies the fact that sexual stimulation makes the vagina rapidly become very wet. The medical controversy revolves around the questions: Is there a female prostate? Are female sexual fluids released through the urethra?

Let us look at the evidence of widespread popular belief in the reality of female ejaculation. Language itself, generally one of the most permanent repositories of ideas—and of the thoughts people in a given place in a given time had about those ideas—reveals a great deal about what was known a century or more ago about the female sexual fluids. For example, the verb used in Victorian England to describe the climax of sexual excitement was "to spend." And the same word—"spending"—was used for the sexual climax of both men and women, just as we today use the term "to come." Both, of course, are references to the spending and coming of the fluids. A more contemporary term is "to have an orgasm," but here, too, one finds that the word "orgasm" is derived from a Greek verb that means "to swell with moisture."

For a long period of time, the little lips of the

vagina were commonly known as the "nymphae"—a name thought to have been introduced by Colombo in the sixteenth century, but used in the first century by Rufus (see page 14).

Nymphae means "water goddesses" in Greek. Since the little lips, or labia minora, surround the woman's glans and the urethral opening through which the prostatic fluid comes out, the choice of the name is an apt one. Dickinson refers to the ancient practice in Greek comedy of male actors who played the parts of women wearing "bags of fluid to denote genital excitement."* The ancient Greeks were well aware that women ejaculated fluids and that these fluids were particularly observable at the peak of excitement.† They often referred to young brides as "nymphs," indicating an association between brides and fluids.

In Japanese, which is in all other respects a language very different from Greek, one comes across the same association in a popular two-line poem: "The bride is never dry/None [of us] knows why." In phrase after phrase, the Japanese language uninhibitedly documents recognition of the phenomenon of female ejaculation. For example, the Japanese word for coitus is *nure*, meaning "to grow wet." From the root word *nure*, two other terms are derived: *nuregoto*, a term used on the Japanese stage, which means sexual liaison or intercourse, or, literally, "a

*Robert Latou Dickinson, *Human Sex Anatomy*, 2nd ed. (Baltimore: The Williams & Wilkins Company, 1949), p. 48.

†See Translators' Notes in H. B. Jocelyn and B. P. Setchell, trans., Regnier de Graaf, *New Treatise Concerning the Generative Organs of Women*, 1672, *Journal of Reproduction and Fertility*, 77–222 (Oxford: Blackwell Scientific Publications, 1972), Supplement 17, Note 186, p. 200.

thing that renders one wet," and *nuregoke,* "a moist [loose] widow." There is no question that these words refer to wetness from the female genitals. And Dickinson has also noted that it was "the habit of the famous artists of the popular Japanese woodcut to depict [female secretions] pouring forth."*

A few months after I was married I lived for a while in a fellaheen village in the Nile Delta, working with my husband. As the only female member of a village redevelopment team, I had the opportunity to share the female life of the community, which was off limits to the men. What I discovered, with a newly acquired and very limited vocabulary in colloquial Arabic, was a surprising earthiness about sexual matters among these women who lived "behind the veil"—a quality of theirs as unexpected to me as perhaps my own obvious embarrassment was to them. Some of the more specific details that came up in my conversations with them are evidently typical of women in general in the Muslim world, as I later found confirmed in an excerpt from a book by Paul Vieille about women in that culture: "The woman is not perceived as a being having a specific sexuality. Her internal organs are seen as like those of a man; she is seen as ejaculating, but she is not seen, as are boys, as having an autonomous sexual life."†

Many of us who read the *Kama Sutra* tend to have high expectations of the openness about sex in

*Dickinson, *op. cit.,* p. 48. See Friedrich Krauss, *Das Geschlechtleben in Glauben, Sitte und Brauch der Japaner* (Leipzig: Deutsche Verlagsactiengesellsdraft, 1907).

†Paul Vieille, "Iranian Women in Family Alliance and Sexual Politics," in Lois Beck and Nikki Keddie, eds., *Women in the Muslim World* (Cambridge, Mass.: Harvard University Press, 1978), p. 463.

Indian culture. Anyone who visits India, however, soon learns that when it comes to women, it is a country of very decided sexual reserve. Yet in a book about the differences between Hindu and Buddhist Tantras, the subject of female ejaculation is explicitly discussed in a quite matter-of-fact fashion: "Usually the great pleasure of a female is much more than [that of the] male; her ejaculation is much later. The ejaculation of the female . . . is slow, the male is fast."*

Buried in the psychology journals of forty years ago, references to female ejaculation can be found in cultures as far apart as those of the Mohave Indians of the American West and the Trukese, who inhabit a small group of coral islands in the South Pacific. One article, by George Devereux, a proponent of psychoanalytical theory, reports that the Mohave believe women ejaculate. On the basis of the evidence he collected, he concludes that Mohave women expel some kind of fluid not only during coitus, but also while engaging in fellatio or anal coitus. He notes too that the Mohave believe the moisture observable in a woman's vagina after coitus is the product of her own ejaculation, and goes on to explain, "hence, some jealous husbands examine the genitals of their wives for traces of excessive moisture, which would prove she had committed adultery in his absence."†

The Trukese similarly believe that women expel fluids during sexual activity. In one of their studies of the sexual behavior of the Trukese, anthropolo-

*Chien-Ming Chen, *Discriminations Between Buddhist and Hindu Tantras* (Kalimpong, India: Maui Publishing Works, 1969; Harvard-Yenching Institute Library), pp. 13, 201, 202.

†George Devereux, "Mohave Orality," *Psychoanalytic Quarterly,* 16: 539, 1947.

gists T. Gladwin and S. B. Sarason report: "Coitus is phrased by several of our informants as a contest between the man and the woman, a matter of the man restraining his orgasm until the woman has achieved hers. Female orgasm is commonly signaled by urination, although failing this a woman still gives adequate indication of its onset."* This information was passed along from other scholars in the area. Devereux confirms that the Trukese and other Micronesians believe that a woman's sexual response is characterized by "urination before and during the climax" and that this act is apparently equated in their minds with ejaculation. In his article, Devereux also cites the German anthropologist Otto Finsch, who studied the native Ponapese of the South Pacific: "If a Ponapese man wishes to impregnate his principal wife, he first stimulates her to the point where she urinates and then only proceeds to have intercourse with her."†

With the knowledge that we now have about the female prostatic glands and their function, there can be little doubt that the female fluid the Mohave Indians, Trukese, and Ponapese thought was urine is actually fluid from the female prostate. Even in our own culture, the two fluids have usually been confused.

Other references to female ejaculation are to be

*T. Gladwin, and S. B. Sarason, *Truk: Man in Paradise* (New York: Wenner-Gren Foundation for Anthropological Research, 1953), p. 109.

†Otto Finsch, "Über die Einwohner der Insel Ponape (b'stl. Carolinen)," *Zeitschrift für Ethnologie,* 12:301–332, 1880, cited in George Devereux, "The Significance of the External Female Genitalia and of Female Orgasm for the Male," *Journal of American Psychoanalytic Association,* 6:282, 1958.

found in books by authors who themselves deny the authenticity of the phenomenon. In *The Other Victorians: A Study of Sexuality and Pornography in Mid-Nineteenth Century England,* Steven Marcus writes, "Certain of the similarities between *My Secret Life* (1888) and pornographic writings are worth considering. There is first the ubiquitous projection of the male sexual fantasy onto the female response," including "the usual accompanying fantasy that they ejaculate during orgasm."* And in *Eros Denied: Sex in Western Society,* Wayland Young writes that in the past "women were thought to diffuse an actual fecund fluid at the moment of orgasm exactly as men ejaculated. The old erotic books are full of descriptions of the mingling of these vital fluids"—though he himself does not believe that women ejaculate.†

Science generally recognizes that although much knowledge is certainly uncovered by observation, reasoning, and testing, more knowledge—much more—always remains "hidden by the dusky night of nature, uninterrogated."‡ In the case of the female prostate, the subject has been thoroughly investigated in the past, but the resulting medical informa-

*Steven Marcus, *The Other Victorians: A Study of Sexuality and Pornography in Mid-Nineteenth Century England* (New York: Basic Books, 1966), p. 194.

†Wayland Young, *Eros Denied: Sex in Western Society* (New York: Grove Press, 1964), p. 296.

‡These are the words of Sir William Harvey (1578–1657), famous for his discovery of the circulation of the blood. Harvey, the physician of Francis Bacon, also had a lifelong interest in reproduction and the origins of life. His investigative methods set the stage for the modern scientific method—and this in a time when, except for the giants like Harvey himself, Bacon, Galileo, and a few others, the practices of "science" were still very close to those of magic.

tion has become obscure. Nonetheless, the evidence, though dispersed, does exist; and, using the resources of several university library systems, including Harvard's vast holdings, I was able to track it down and bring this lost knowledge to light in a 1976 research paper.*

First and foremost among the numerous physicians whose works scientifically validate the existence of a female prostate is the Dutch anatomist Regnier de Graaf. Three hundred years ago in his treatise on the generative organs of women,† de Graaf presented accurate drawings and descriptions of the glandular structure around the female urethra (Figure 25), identified this structure as the female prostate, and described it as the source of the highly erotic female sexual fluids:

> The urethra is lined internally by a thin membrane. In the lower part, near the outlet of the urinary passage, this membrane is pierced by large ducts, or lacunae, through which pituito-serous matter occasionally discharges in considerable quantities.
>
> Between this very thin membrane and the fleshy fibres we have just described, there is, along the whole duct of the urethra, a whitish, membranous substance about one finger-breadth thick which completely surrounds the urethral

*Josephine Lowndes Sevely, "Female Ejaculation" (unpublished paper, Harvard University, 1976).

†Regnier de Graaf, *New Treatise Concerning the Generative Organs of Women,* 1672, in H. B. Jocelyn and B. P. Setchell, trans., *Journal of Reproduction and Fertility,* Supplement 17 (Oxford: Blackwell Scientific Publications, 1972), pp. 77–222.

canal. . . . The substance could be called quite aptly the female prostatae or corpus glandulosum, "glandulous body." It seems to us too to be what Galen is talking about when, in Book 14 of his work on the use of the parts, he writes, on the authority of Herophilus, that women as well as men have glandulous "prostatae."

The function of the "prostate" is to generate a pituito-serous juice which makes women more libidinous with its pungency and saltiness and lubricates their sexual parts in agreeable fashion during coitus. . . .

Before we continue further, it occurs to us that we should mention that there are many tiny pores all along the canal of the vagina. They are largest and most numerous at the bottom of the vagina near the outlet of the urinary passage. Here they are often as large as those in the urinary passage which we described above and named lacunae or ducts. From all the vaginal ducts, big and small, sero-pituitous matter flows in sufficient quantity to keep the genital parts moist. During the sexual act it discharges to lubricate the tract so copiously that it even flows outside the pudenda. This is the matter which many have taken to be actual female semen.

Here too it should be noted that the discharge from the female "prostatae" causes as much pleasure as does that from the male "prostatae."

De Graaf also notes that women can be stirred to this pleasure by "frisky fingers," and that "in libidinous women," the liquid "often rushes out at the mere sight of a handsome man."*

*De Graaf, (67, 68, 80, 81, 213) *op. cit.,* pp. 103, 104, 106, 107, 141.

I represents a urethra or urinary passage opened
   lengthwise in the front part

    A *urinary bladder*
    B *neck of the bladder opened*
    C *urethra opened lengthwise*
    D *orifice of the urethra and exits of the lacunae in it*
    E *lacunae traversing the "prostatae"*
    F *lacunae taken from the "prostatae" and*
       distended by air
    G *internal substance of the "prostatae"*
       or glandulous body
    H *parts of the bladder drawn apart after division*
    I *ureters cut*
    K *labia of the pudendum*
    L *orifice of the vagina*
    M *fleshy fibers of the sphincter cut*

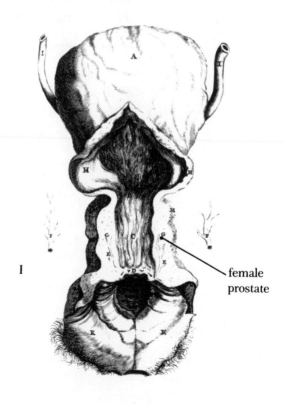

I

female
prostate

II shows the space between the urethra and the vagina

A *urinary bladder*
B *ureters cut*
C *neck of the bladder opened*
D *urethra divided through the middle*
E *blind apertures of the lacunae, or ducts, traversing the "prostatae"*
F *lacunae traversing the "prostatae"*
G *length and thickness of the "prostatae" or glandulous body between the urethra and the vagina*
H *length and thickness of the "prostatae" above the urethra*
I *parts of the bladder drawn apart*
K *inner surface of the urinary bladder*
L *wrinkled substance of the vagina*
M *orifice of the vagina*
N *labia of the pudendum*

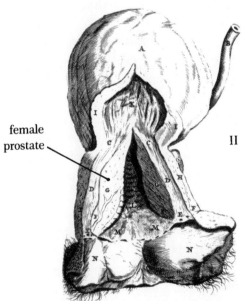

female prostate

II

FIG. 25 Drawings of the Glandular Structure Around the Female Urethra (*Above figure is shown at two thirds original size*) (*Regnier de Graaf, 1672*)

Whether or not current research findings will validate all of de Graaf's ideas, it behooves us to focus attention on his research and reasoning in his attempt to resolve a question still under study in our our times:

> There will doubtless be critics who, believing that the liquid which rushes out with such impetus during venereal combat or libidinous imagining is semen, will enquire whence this liquid comes and for what purpose it is designed. We think that it comes primarily from the lacunae in the orifices of the vagina and urinary tract and secondarily from the large number of passages in the cervix. The pores in the vagina and the inner part of the uterus doubtless also make some contribution.
>
> Someone will enquire further whence these ducts or lacunae draw this fluid. The first-mentioned ducts, namely those which are visible around the orifice of the neck of the vagina and the outlet of the urinary passage, receive their fluid from the female "prostate," or rather the thick membranous body around the urinary passage. The second-mentioned ducts collect their liquid from the nervous and membranous substance of the neck of the uterus. The rest of the liquid which flows out through the pores of the uterus and the vagina comes from the membranous and perhaps also from the glandulous substance of these parts. . . .
>
> The liquid about which we have spoken does not come from the "testicles" or the tubes. The "testicles" do not contain one quarter as much liquid as usually comes from the pudenda in one

gush, so to speak (as experts in this matter have informed me).*

In his definitive article on the female prostatic glands, gynecologist J.W. Huffman traces the history of the anatomy of these glands back to the anatomist Herophilus in the third century B.C.† He also mentions Galen's reference to a female prostate gland, stating his own belief that Galen may have been alluding to some structure other than the gland about the urethra. A careful reading of Galen's own words leads one to believe that he probably was confused about the anatomical source of the fluid and definitely wrong in calling the fluid "semen," but was acute in his actual description of the fluid itself. Almost all the early anatomists took for granted that Galen was talking about the female prostate, but they disagreed with his idea that there is a homologue of the male prostate in the female. Only Picolomini (1526–1605) agreed with him. Huffman credits de Graaf with the first scientific description of the glands and ducts that surround the female urethra.

Of the following eighteen anatomical studies Huffman goes on to cite, fourteen corroborate the existence of a female prostate, and only four deny it:

*De Graaf, *op. cit.,* p. 141. Early anatomists commonly used the term "testicles" for either the male or female gonads. Although de Graaf uses the undifferentiating term here for the female, he was the scientist who later in the same treatise pointed out that in women the "testicles" should be called "ovaries."

†J.W. Huffman, "The Detailed Anatomy of the Paraurethral Ducts in the Adult Human Female," *American Journal of Obstetrics and Gynecology,* 55: 86–101, 1948.

Astrue (1737), who also described a female prostate and small lacunae (openings); Winslow (1775), who identified smaller lacunae and one larger duct; Boyer (1797), who described the openings of secretory glands in the meatus and urethral lining; Cruweilheir (1844), who denied that a female prostate existed but declared that numerous lacunae did open into the urethral lining; Virchow (1853), who alluded to these glands as the homologue of the male prostate; Robin and Cadiat (1874), who found no glands and doubted the existence of any prostatic homologue; Skene (1880), who identified only two ducts just inside the urethral opening (which had been identified by de Graaf two centuries earlier, but which are still called Skene's ducts); Tourneaux (1889), who again called attention to these glands as homologues of the male prostate; Oberdieck (1884) and later Aschoff (1894), who identified deep prostatic-like lacunae along the urethra; Felix (1912), who agreed that the glandular structure around the urethra is a prostatic homologue; Pallin (1901), who, like Galen, had ideas about the specific portion of the male prostate of which the female glands are the homologue; Wyatt (1911), who concluded that the female glands are indeed prostatic homologues; Johnson (1922), who constructed his own wax models to demonstrate that the ducts around the female urethra are unquestionably homologous with male prostatic ducts; Hunner (1907), who described the openings of numerous mucous glands along the inferior urethral wall and noted that the glands tend to increase in size and complexity toward the outer end of the urethra, and who quoted Schuller (1883) as having found a third but smaller gland or tubule lying in the midline between the two described by Skene.

Huffman continues:

> In recent years, interest has been renewed in this problem, and some disagreement has occurred relative to the presence of urethral glands, other than Skene's ducts, and as to their extent and importance. Deter, Caldwell, and Folsom [1946] have presented evidence that there are tubular glands about the posterior urethra and that they are clinically important in urethral disease. MacKinsie and Beck [1936] after examining numerous longitudinally sectioned urethrae of children and adults reported that true urethral glands do not exist in that third of the urethra nearest the bladder. They found that while the paraurethral glands may encircle the urethra they drain only through openings on the urethral floor. According to MacKinsie and Beck, true periurethral tubular epithelial structures appear in the anterior two-thirds of the urethra adjacent to the compound racemose glands of Skene. These, they feel, are distinct from Skene's ducts, are not always present, and are less frequent in the middle third of the urethra. Cabot and Shoemaker [1936], after studying a number of female urethras cut in longitudinal section, came to the conclusion that there are no important gland structures in the proximal two-thirds of the female urethra; and that glands of the female urethra—except Skene's glands—do not play an important role in infections of the female urinary tract.*

*J. W. Huffman, op. cit., p. 87.

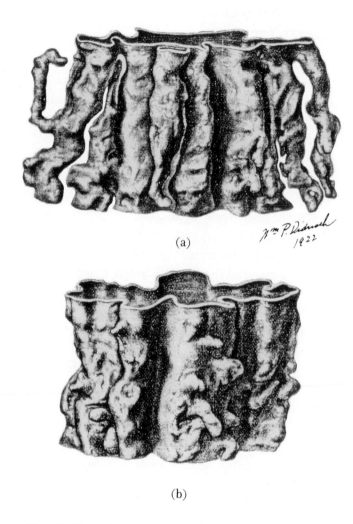

(a)

(b)

FIG. 26 Homologue of the Prostate in the Female: drawings of wax model of two segments of the urethra of a female fetus—(a) distal portion; (b) proximal portion (F. P. Johnson, Journal of Urology 8: 13–24, 1922)

Huffman's own research contributes significantly to our knowledge of the glands and ducts of the adult female urethra, and his anatomical wax models provide evidence in support of those scientists throughout the centuries who, like de Graaf, were convinced that a female prostate is not only part of the normal female anatomy but also is without question a homologue of the male prostate. Other doctors expressed their fear that the name "female prostate" might lead to an overly enthusiastic adoption of the clinical concept of prostatism and tempt clinicians to resort to surgical removal of the glands. For this reason only, Huffman conceded in closing that he could see where it would perhaps be better not to use the term, at least in clinical medicine. On the other hand, a number of the physicians cited by Huffman felt differently. Deter, Caldwell, and Folsom, for example, state:

> The name "female prostate gland" could be used instead of "female peri-urethral glands" in order to emphasize the homology of these glands in the male and female, in the same way as the name "utriculus masculinus" is used to show that this gland is homologous with the uterus of the female.*

I use the term "female ejaculation" in the same way, to emphasize the fact that the sexual function of these corresponding glandular structures in men and women is similar. Since one of the themes of this

*R. L. Deter, G. T. Caldwell, and A. I. Folsom, "A Clinical and Pathological Study of the Posterior Female Urethra," *Journal of Urology* 55: 653, 1946.

book is the close symmetry between the two sexes' sexual organs, both terms seem appropriate. Because the interest of most physicians in the female prostate has been of a clinical nature, the emphasis has been on disorders and treatment of the female urethra. As a result, the medical profession by and large has been much less outspoken about female ejaculation. Ample evidence of the phenomenon can, nevertheless, be found in the scientific literature (Figures 27–30).

In 1926 Dr. Theodoor H. Van de Velde, the internationally famous Dutch gynecologist, published his book on the sexual life of men and women. In it, a

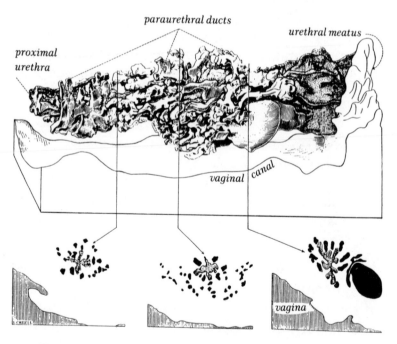

FIG. 27 Adult Human Female Urethra (Model I): drawing based on a wax model showing paraurethral ducts and glands; see Fig. 21 (*J. W. Huffman, 1948*)

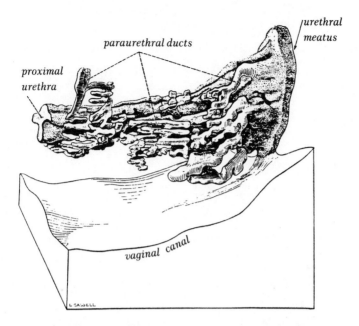

FIG. 28 Adult Human Female Urethra with Paraurethral Ducts (Model II): drawing of a wax model; tissues obtained at necropsy of a thirty-eight-year-old woman who had never given birth (*J.W. Huffman, 1948*)

work that had the unqualified support of the medical profession, Dr. Van de Velde addressed the question:

> But what of ejaculation? So far as I can form an opinion on this subject, it appears that the majority of laymen believe that something is forcibly squirted (or propelled or extruded), or expelled from the woman's body in orgasm, and should so happen normally, as in the man's case. Finally, it is at least just as certain that such an "ejaculation" does not take place in many women of sexually normal functions, as that it does take place in others.*

*T. H. Van de Velde, *Ideal Marriage: Its Physiology and Technique* (New York: Random House, 1957), pp. 195, 196.

((*81*))

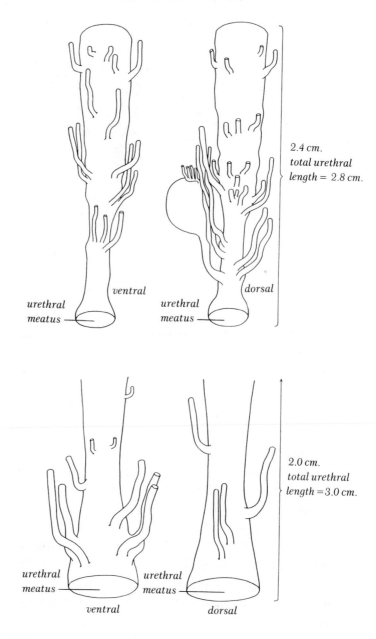

FIG. 29 View of Paraurethral Ducts Showing Their Distribution: diagrams of Models I and II (*J.W. Huffman,* *1948*)

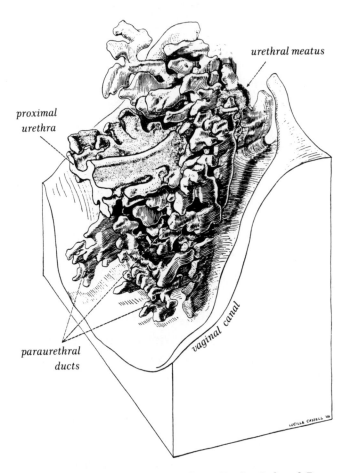

Fig. 30 Ventro-lateral View from Right Side of Paraurethral Ducts and Glands (Model III): drawings of a
wax model; tissues obtained at necropsy of a thirty-two-
year-old virgin (*J. W. Huffman, 1948*)

Writing in 1929, the physician G. V. Hamilton informed his readers:

The word "orgasm" is used to designate the spas-
modic, highly pleasurable feeling with which the
sex act ends for both men and women. Men often
use the term "going off" to designate this part of

the sex act, and with them it is accompanied by the discharge of semen. Women do not discharge semen at such time, of course, but with that exception their orgasm or "going off" is essentially similar to that of men.*

The famous psychologist Havelock Ellis described in 1937 the observations of some gynecologists that during pelvic examinations an occasional patient would ejaculate a fluid that was "sometimes described as being emitted in a jet which is thrown to a distance."†

One of the most invaluable contributions to the study of human sexuality and sexual anatomy is that of gynecologist Robert Latou Dickinson. A case study from his records provides a detailed description of female ejaculation. The reported subject was twenty-two, the happily married mother of a son aged one and a half. Dickinson includes a physical description: five feet five inches tall, deep brown eyes, fair skin, classic Grecian features, very feminine in appearance. The young woman started masturbating at age nine by running water from the faucet onto her genitals. The practice led to clitoral manipulation to the point of orgasm. She herself referred to these orgasms as "bladder orgasms," because as a child she had assumed that the accompanying ejaculation of fluid was urine. "Most of the time," Dickinson writes, "masturbation was unpremeditated. But when the

*G. V. Hamilton, *A Research on Marriage* (New York: Boni, 1929), p. 25.

†Havelock Ellis, *Studies in the Psychology of Sex,* Vol. 3 (New York: Random House, 1936), p. 146.

folks were away, she would also make preparations for it, which included a towel, so the ejaculation would not get on the bed. After several orgasms, another orgasm would produce a sort of ejaculation varying from a very small amount to quite a large amount."* The sequence described matches anecdotal reports from other women and from their partners who have shared the experience. Characteristically, the ejaculating woman experiences one or two orgasms—or a heightening of sensation very close to orgasm—before the orgasm that brings on an expulsion of fluid.

Despite references to female ejaculation such as these, awareness of the female prostate as a source of sexual fluids or of de Graaf's early depiction of the erotic nature of the female urethra seems to have been lost for a period in time. It was not until 1950 that another physician, Dr. Ernest Grafenberg, reported his observation of the expulsion of female sexual fluids from the urethra:

> Some investigators of female sex behavior believe that most women cannot experience vaginal orgasm, because there are no nerves in the vaginal wall. In contrast to this statement by Kinsey, Hardenberg mentions that nerves have been demonstrated only inside the vagina in the anterior wall, proximate to the base of the clitoris. This I can confirm by my own experience of numerous women. An erotic zone always could be demonstrated on the anterior wall of the vagina along

*From the personal papers of Robert Latou Dickinson, M.D., Francis A. Countway Library of Medicine, Harvard University. Used by permission.

the course of the urethra. . . . Analogous to the male urethra, the female urethra also seems to be surrounded by erectile tissues like the corpora cavernosa. In the course of sexual stimulation, the female urethra begins to enlarge and can be felt easily. It swells out greatly at the end of orgasm. . . . Occasionally the production of fluids is so profuse that a large towel has to be spread under the woman to prevent the bedsheets getting soiled. This convulsory expulsion of fluids occurs always at the acme of the orgasm and simultaneously with it. If there is the opportunity to observe the orgasm of such women, one can see that large quantities of a clear transparent fluid are expelled not from the vulva, but out of the urethra in gushes. At first I thought that the bladder sphincter had become defective by the intensity of the orgasm. Involuntary expulsion of urine is reported in sex literature. In the cases observed by us, the fluid was examined and it had no urinary character. . . . This short paper will, I hope, show that the anterior wall of the vagina along the urethra is the seat of a distinct erotogenic zone and has to be taken into account more in the treatment of female sexual deficiency.*

Cultural and medical corroboration of the phenomenon of female ejaculation abounds, but the leading contemporary authorities nevertheless deny that women ejaculate. Alfred Kinsey, for example, was well aware of the reports of female ejaculation in the medical literature, and cites the descriptions of it by Van de Velde, Ellis, and Grafenberg. He also

*Ernest Grafenberg, "The Role of the Urethra in Female Orgasm," *The International Journal of Sexology,* 1950, 3: pp. 146, 147, 148.

knew of the popular acceptance of the phenomenon, noting, "The expulsion of genital secretions by the female at orgasm, which is the so-called 'female ejaculation,' is popularly known and talked about."* But Kinsey then goes on to state: "Orgasm in the female matches the orgasm of the male in every physiologic detail except for the fact that it occurs without ejaculation."† In their studies, William Masters and Virginia Johnson identify the male sexual response with simultaneous orgasm and ejaculation, whereas the female response is limited to orgasm. They, like Kinsey, deny the existence of female ejaculation— this despite the fact that a number of their own subjects reported sensation of fluids being ejaculated during orgasm:

> During the first stage of subjective progression in orgasm, the sensation of intense clitoral-pelvic awareness has been described by a number of women as occurring concomitantly with a sense of bearing down or expelling. Often a feeling of receptive opening was expressed. This last sensation was reported only by parous study subjects, a small number of whom expressed some concept of having an actual fluid emission or of expending in some concrete fashion. Previous male interpretation of these subjective reports may have resulted in the erroneous but widespread concept that female ejaculation is an integral part of female orgasmic expression.‡

*A. C. Kinsey, W. B. Pomeroy, C. E. Martin, and P. H. Gebhard, *Sexual Behavior in the Human Female* (Philadelphia and London: W. B. Saunders Company, 1953), pp. 634, 635.

†Ibid.

‡William H. Masters and Virginia E. Johnson, *Human Sexual Response* (Boston: Little, Brown and Company, 1966), p. 135.

Just as fads in sexual physiology have in the past focused attention on one excitatory spot or another in the female anatomy, so too ideas about the source of female sexual fluids have tended to focus on one specific fluid or another in a given period. In 1675, three years after the publication of de Graaf's treatise identifying the female sexual fluids as fluids from the prostatic glands of the urethra, the Danish physician Caspar Bartholin discovered the glands that to this day bear his name. It gradually came to be thought that Bartholin's discovery served to "correct" de Graaf's ideas about the source of the female sexual fluids. Later when it was determined, however, that these glands do not significantly contribute to female sexual fluids but rather supply only a few drops of liquid near the vaginal entrance, ideas about the source of the fluids shifted to the vagina, making cervical fluids the focus of interest as they had been in the past. Many a twentieth-century physician, including the knowledgeable gynecologist Dickinson, assumed that the sexual secretions found in women came from the cervix. The cervix was, however, eliminated as the supposed source of "vaginal lubrication" as a result of sexual stimulation when William Masters, in a 1959 study of the subject,* reported that a pronounced vaginal sweating reaction had been observed repeatedly in a subject who had had her uterus and both her ovaries removed.

Masters's theory, which was the next to prevail, proposed that the fluids were produced by a process of diffusion through the vaginal walls, but this the-

*William H. Masters, "The Sexual Response Cycle of the Human Female: Vaginal Lubrication," *Annals of New York Academy of Sciences* 83: 303, 1959.

ory identified the mechanism of production, not the source of the fluids. According to Masters, the source remained a mystery. No one recalled that the "discredited" de Graaf had correctly identified the female prostate as one of the main sources. In his perceptive early work, de Graaf was also able to determine that "there are many tiny pores all along the canal of the vagina." These pores, which he was somehow able to detect with the naked eye, were only recently uncovered with the help of a powerful scanning electron microscope—a tribute to de Graaf's perception as a scientist.*

It is now possible to present a much more comprehensive idea of the sources of female sexual fluids. The female ejaculate is actually made up of a number of different fluids from different parts of the urogenital system. They include: the so-called transudate across the lining of the upper vagina; cervical mucus; fluids from the endometrium of the uterus; Fallopian tube fluid; secretions from sebaceous and sweat glands in the vulval area; the fluid from the two Bartholin ducts; and—the major component, according to de Graaf's findings, from which my theory

---

*There is an outside chance that de Graaf might have had access to very early versions of microscopic lenses developed by Anthony Leuwenhoeck, since they both lived in the town of Delft. Also de Graaf brought Leuwenhoeck's work to the attention of the Royal Society of London, reported in *Philosophical Transactions of the Royal Society,* 8: 6037–8, 1673.

For the modern studies, see H. Ludwig, and H. Metzger, *The Human Female Reproductive Tract: A Scanning Electron Microscopic Atlas* (Berlin: Springer-Verlag, 1976), and M. H. Burgos and R. deVargas-Linares, "Cell Junctions in the Human Vaginal Epithelium," *American Journal of Obstetrics and Gynecology,* 108: 565, 1970.

has been developed—fluid from the prostatic glands ejaculated through the urethral opening.*

The new glandular theory proposes that prostatic glands exist in every human, male and female. The function of these glands in the female is affected by genetic factors which determine size, the number of ducts, and the sensitivity of the tissues. Other factors that have to be considered in studying the performance of these glands are age, aging, and possibly the same kind of conditioning of reflexes that affects the functioning of other glands in the human body.† For example, the prostatic action may be tempered by the extent of stimulation from the "squeezing" of the gland and by the extent of use. But by far the most significant variable affecting the creation of fluid is the psychological one.

The following excerpt from de Graaf's description of the female prostate indicates that he knew this long before psychology existed as a discipline. "Reason persuades us, and experience confirms," he

*See G. Preti, G. R. Huggins, and G. D. Silverberg, "Alterations in the Organic Compounds of Vaginal Secretions Caused by Sexual Arousal," *Fertility Sterility,* 32 (1): 47–54, 1979; R. O. Raffi, L. S. Moghiss, and A. G. Sacco, "Proteins of Human Vaginal Fluid," *Fertility Sterility,* 28: 1345, 1977; L. Cohen, "Influence of pH on Vaginal Discharges," *British Journal of Venereal Disease,* 45: 241, 1969; W. H. Masters, "The Sexual Response Cycle of the Human Female: Vaginal Lubrication," *Annals of New York Academy of Science,* 83: 301–17, 1959; J. B. Doyle, F. J. Ewers, and D. Sapit, "The New Fertility Testing Tape: A Predictive Test of the Fertile Period," *Journal of American Medical Association,* 172: 1744, 1960; and E.S.E. Hafez, and D. L. Black, "The Mammalian Uterotubal Junction," in E.S.E. Hafez and D. L. Black, eds., *The Mammalian Oviduct: Comparative Biology and Methodology* (Chicago: University of Chicago Press, 1969).

†See also p. 46.

writes (without stating whose experience), "that the liquid which moistens the male member and the pubis during sexual intercourse . . . in libidinous women often rushes out at the mere sight of a handsome man." Also an allusion to female ejaculation may be discerned in a phrase in Shakespeare's *All's Well That Ends Well* (Act I, sc. iii), in which the yearning Helena, speaking of her unrequited love for Bertram, refers to "the waters of my love." More recently, Fritz Mohr, a psychologist who wrote in the 1920s, after alluding to the experiments of I. P. Pavlov and R. R. Heyer that demonstrated the importance of psychological factors in oral secretions, proceeds to state that the "increase or decrease of genital secretion in healthy girls and women as a result of psychic influence goes without saying."[*]

According to the new glandular theory, all women normally ejaculate sexual fluids from the prostatic glands. Ejaculation and orgasm are physiologically distinct, and no evidence exists of any correlation between the specifics of the two different phenomena. Men and women vary as to the frequency of ejaculation and the volume of fluid produced.

We have conducted a study to determine the amounts of female fluid produced during sexual stimulation. Volunteer subjects, using a preferred method of self-stimulation, collected the fluids in the privacy of their own surroundings. Each participant agreed to refrain from contact with sperm for three days before carrying out a medically approved procedure for collection of the fluids. After emptying the

[*]Fritz Mohr, *Psychophysische Behandlungsmethoden* (Leipzig: Hirzel, 1925), p. 509.

bladder and washing the genital area, the subject inserted a diaphragm over the cervix and tampons inside the vagina. Specimens of urethral fluid were collected directly in plastic containers, which were then frozen until brought to the laboratory. The tampons were removed, placed in plastic containers, and similarly frozen until dispatched to the laboratory. To help control any possible influencing of the results and also to protect the subjects' anonymity, each container had been pre-numbered and confidentially recorded under the subject's name.

As a result of a case study, we have been able to determine that during sexual excitement the amount of prostatic fluid released through the female urethra may be as much as 126 milliliters (about one quarter of a cup, or four ounces). Compared to the volume of prostatic fluids, the amount of fluid produced inside the vagina by the same subject during the same period is negligible.

We have also tested the prostatic fluid for urea. It is known that the normal range of value for urea in urine may be as high as 15 grams per liter of urine, but rarely less than 5 grams per liter. The results we obtained, however, showed that the urea in the female prostatic fluid is at a much lower range—1.3–3.9 grams per liter. The fact that the urea level in this fluid is less than the normal range for urine suggests that it is not urine.

Among most women, any sexual fluid that is expressed is immediately taken to be vaginal fluid. The association is understandable for a number of reasons. In the past, the only fluids ever mentioned by the authorities were always designated "vaginal" fluids. Furthermore, the fluids from the prostatic glands, because they are ejaculated through the ure-thral opening which is in close proximity to the opening of the vagina, appear to be coming from the vagina. In an anatomical case study conducted in order to observe the functional relationship between the urethra and the vagina, a glass cylinder one and a half inches in diameter was introduced into the vagina to stimulate penile interaction with the ure-thra. The photographic records of the positions of the anatomical parts clearly show that the urethral meatus—through which the fluids are ejaculated—is pushed inside the vagina beyond the pubic arch. In the process, the Lowndes crown is drawn down to the vagina. The study demonstrates that, although the woman's glans appears to be more or less "fixed" in position, it is capable of a range of excursion suffi-cient to permit some movement in and out of the vagina—which may help to explain why many women think they do not ejaculate. If a woman ejaculates fluid only during coitus, the outlet of the fluid is obscured inside the vagina; and since the ejaculation cannot be observed, the fluid is perceived as merely increased wetness in the vagina. But if the sexual response is elicited by means other than coi-tus, and the woman's glans is unobstructed, the ejac-ulation of fluid can usually be seen as a series of "spurts" or "jets," as frequently described in reports like the ones previously cited.

Another factor that may make it difficult for a woman to recognize when she is experiencing an ejaculation has to do with the number and organiza-tion of the female ducts. In the male, the fluid from the prostate is ejaculated through only two ducts im-mediately before entering the urethra, thus putting

EVE'S SECRETS

the fluid under relatively great pressure. In the female, the fluid is ejaculated into the urethra through as many as *thirty-one* ducts scattered along its length, so that the fluid pressure is more diffused.

Finally, in his definitive anatomical study showing the fusion of the lower urethra and the roof of the vagina, Dr. Kermit E. Krantz mentions that the female urethra, upon the willed contraction of the sphincter muscle, rises in and upward into the vagina.* This action, one within the voluntary control of the woman, is another factor that would tend to make ejaculation difficult to observe.

In other forms of sexual activity—for example, cunnilingus or digital stimulation of the genitals, during which the woman's glans is not continuously obstructed as it is in coitus—the "rush" of fluids can, as we have noted, be observed coming out of the urethral opening. Men have anecdotally reported seeing female ejaculation as "a circular shower of jets" (when the woman was in a standing position) or as "two fine, angular intermittent jets" (when the woman was reclining). These descriptions fit the type of ejaculation that occurs during heightened excitement. Female prostatic fluids, however, can also be observed coming out of the urethra during the initial stages of excitement as well, when genital wetness first occurs—something de Graaf somehow knew. At this stage of excitement the urethral fluids "gush" rather than "spurt"—presumably because they are under less pressure than at a later stage of excitation and built-up orgasmic tension.

*Kermit E. Krantz, "The Anatomy of the Urethra and Anterior Vaginal Wall," *Transactions of the American Association of Obstetrics, Gynecology, and Abdominal Surgery,* 61: 31, 1950.

The relatively profuse prostatic fluid can easily be distinguished from the very scant Bartholin fluid released early on. The latter fluid is thicker and relatively sticky, whereas the prostatic fluid is a clear, glycerine-like substance. Dickinson observes that the most frequent evidence of roused female sexual desire—though by no means, one should interject, the *only* evidence—is the expression of sexual fluids. Dickinson was wrong in thinking that this fluid came from the cervix or the Bartholin glands. All the same, he provides us with a description that exactly fits the characteristics of female prostatic fluid: "clear as glass, tenacious and persistent, without being sticky."

In making this observation, Dickinson relied on his own senses. The thoroughgoing de Graaf, on the other hand, while he depended on the faculties of sight and touch to describe the fluids, was not averse to conducting trials, as he put it, "before the tribunal of taste," as in the sentence already quoted: "The function of the 'prostate' is to generate a . . . juice which makes women more libidinous with its pungency and saltiness and lubricates their sexual parts in agreeable fashion during coitus."*

The odor of female sexual secretions has been of greater interest to science, because of its possible role in attracting the male. Women themselves report that the fragrance of the fluids is somewhat like that of citrus fruit; the smell of fresh oranges is often mentioned for comparison. Van de Velde compares the fragrance to a sweeter one still, that of a pineapple. In their study of vaginal odors, G. R. Huggins and

*De Graaf (67, 68), *op. cit.*, p. 104. This sentence was also included in the earlier, fuller quotation from de Graaf on page 70.

G. Preti write, "Both anecdotal reports and personal experiences gathered from colleagues suggest that a change in odor of the female genital region occurs during sexual arousal."* They point out, however, that "the reported increase in genital odor during arousal has several potential components, but its significance in terms of endocrine or behavioral changes in males has yet to be determined."

The phenomenon of male ejaculation has always been accepted without question. Historically, as we have seen, certain restrictions were imposed by religious codes that limited its frequency. There were also earlier beliefs that acted as restraints—for example, that coitus unduly sapped a man's vitality and undermined his health, or that excessive masturbation to the point of ejaculation could cause madness.

We have come to realize that ejaculation may be equally normal for both sexes—that, indeed, to try to repress in either sex what is intrinsic in the nature of one's sexuality is to deny both. Falling in love and lovemaking are two of the more fascinating aspects of human life. And a focus of this fascination is, and has been historically, the desire and pleasure associated with the coming of the female fluids.

In a recapitulation of the history of the subject, the French historian Michel Foucault describes

*G. R. Huggins and G. Preti, "Vaginal Odors and Secretions," *Clinical Obstetrics and Gynecology* 24 (1): 370, 372, 1981. See also R. W. Bonzall and R. P. Michael, "Volatile Odoriferous Acids in Vaginal Fluid," in E.S.E. Hafez and T. N. Evans, eds., *The Human Vagina* (Amsterdam and New York: North Holland Publishing Co., 1978), pp. 167–177.

Galen's ideas from almost two thousand years ago.*
The desire and pleasure involved in the coming of
the fluids are, according to Galen, the direct effects of
the way in which the anatomy is arranged and of the
physical processes—an approach that one may call,
Foucault suggests, a "physiologization" of desire and
pleasure. "In this mechanism," Foucault continues,
"Galen sees several factors of pleasure. There is first
of all the accumulation of the body-fluid, the nature
of which is such that it triggers there—where the
body-fluid collects—lively sensations or feelings."†
Galen himself described as one of the characteristics
of the fluid the "particular need of this kind of juice,
which naturally stimulates the parts to act and make
their action pleasurable."‡ Galen goes on to liken it
to the sort of thing that often suddenly happens following the accumulation [and heating] under the
skin of penetrating body-fluids, "the movement of
which excites a titillating and a pleasant longing."§
Foucault further explains Galen's ideas about
pleasure:

> In any case, Nature gave the organs in this area
> a special sensibility, much greater than that of
> the skin, despite their having the same functions.
> Lastly, the much thinner humor [body-fluid] com-
> ing from the glandular bodies Galen calls *para-*
> *statas* constitutes an additional material factor of

*Michel Foucault, *Histoire de la Sexualité: Le Souci de Soi,*
Vol. 3 (Paris: Gallimard, 1984), pp. 129, 130.

†Ibid., p. 130.

‡Galen, *On the Usefulness of the Parts (De usu partium),*
Book 14.9, Vol. II, tr. by Margaret Tallmadge May (Ithaca, N.Y.:
Cornell University Press, 1968), p. 640.

§Foucault, *op. cit.,* p. 130

pleasure. This humor [body-fluid], by permeating the parts involved in the sexual act, makes them more elastic and heightens the pleasure they experience.*

The coming of the female fluids continues to evoke in the woman and her partner the greatest pleasure and intimacy of shared passion. And lovers continue to share the same human longing for this experience, which is "astonishing and beyond words."†

*Michel Foucault, *The Care of the Self,* Vol. 3 of *The History of Sexuality,* tr. by Robert Hurley (New York: Pantheon, 1986), p. 108.

†*op. cit.,* p. 128.

CHAPTER 4

The Vagina

V*agina*, originally a Latin word meaning "sheath" or "scabbard," has been the standard name for the female passageway since the mid-sixteenth century. Before that time, anatomists had not yet made any clear distinction between the passageway and the uterus; so when they spoke of coitus, they spoke of the male putting the penis into the "neck of the uterus" (i.e., the cervix) as though into a scabbard (Figure 31).

In 1561, Fallopio became the first to realize that this concept was confusing the cervix with the passageway. The penis can touch or press upon the cervix, but it cannot enter it. By calling the passageway the "vagina" and thereby drawing attention to the distinction between it and the cervix, Fallopio helped to clarify just where the penis goes when it is inserted inside a woman's body. The name took hold and has been handed down to us with the underlying (male) idea that the vagina is a vessel in the service of the penis.

To this day, the standard view focuses on the reproductive function of the vagina. According to

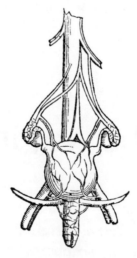

FIG. 31 Drawing of the Uterus (*Vesalius*, The Tabulae Anatomicae Sex, *1538*)

standard medical opinion, the main functions of the vagina are to receive the penis during sexual intercourse and provide a passage for the sperm; to provide a safe passageway for the baby during birth; and to serve as a duct for menstrual fluid.

Alfred Kinsey, et al., in *Sexual Behavior in the Human Female,* present evidence of the erotic insensitivity of the vagina.* Gynecologists conducted two kinds of vaginal tests on 879 females: one for tactile responsiveness, by gently stroking the surface with a probe in four different places—on the anterior surface (the roof of the vagina), the posterior (the floor), and the right and left—and another for awareness of pressure by exerting distinct pressure on the anterior and posterior surfaces with an object described as being larger than a probe. Kinsey recognized that a response to such stimuli did not necessarily indicate

*Kinsey, et al., *op. cit.,* pp. 577, 580.

a woman's capacity for erotic arousal, but a lack of response in a given area of the vagina would tend to indicate the probability that the area could not be involved in erotic response.

The findings revealed that less than 15 percent of these women were, in Kinsey's words, "at all conscious that they had been touched." (His statistical table also indicates, however, that the vagina was highly responsive to pressure, 89 percent of the women having responded to pressure on the roof of the vagina and 93 percent to pressure on its floor.) To support his negative findings, Kinsey mentions other scientists who had done studies (apparently not all of them published at the time) that proved a relative lack of nerves in the vaginal surface, among them Dr. Kermit E. Krantz, who provided Kinsey with data from histological studies.* A medical journal article by Dr. Krantz reported that most women have a rather low sensitivity to pain as well as to touch in most of the vagina, except for the area close to the opening.†

But if one goes back far enough, the Bible recognizes the voluptuousness of the vagina. The text of the Old Testament compiled in the third century B.C. explicitly refers to the sexual cravings of the vagina. Regnier de Graaf quoted the Vulgate, "There are

---

*The others cited were: Dr. F. J. Hector of Bristol, England; A. Kuntz, *The Autonomic Nervous System* (3rd edn., Philadelphia: Lea & Bebiger, 1945); and U. Undeutsch, "Die Sexualitat im Jugendalter," *Studium Generale,* 3: 433–454, 1950.

†K. E. Krantz, "Innervation of the Human Vulva and Vagina: A Microscopic Study," *Obstetrics and Gynecology,* 12: 382–396, 1958.

three things that are never sated ... Hell, the mouth of the vulva [the vagina], and the earth" (Proverbs 30).*

In other cultures, ideas about the vagina's sexual function, and the terms used to describe the part, reflect much more positive attitudes. The ancient Japanese called it "the gate of jewels," because it is said Japanese women up until about the mid-nineteenth century used to carry a pearl inside their vaginas and believed that they would die if it were taken out. According to folk belief, there were not one but three precious stones inside the vagina which moved during coitus.†

Among the Trukese it is the vagina, not the penis, that is the primary symbol of sexuality. A Trukese woman is thought to be able to achieve orgasm and great pleasure for herself and her partner if her vagina is, in their phrase, "full of things." According to an anthropological report sponsored by the U.S. government, these "things" consist of "a prominent clitoris, labia minora, and a small projection below the clitoris whose anatomical definition is unclear."‡ The small projection is presumably the part that we have called the woman's glans.

From the front, a woman's sexual parts appear to be contained within a diamond defined by the pubic

*De Graaf, op. cit. (8), p. 87.

†In the folk language of English-speaking people, one comes across the term "the family jewels," but this is a term reserved for the testicles, connoting the importance of the reproductive function of those male organs.

‡Gladwin and Sarason, Truk: Man in Paradise, p. 109. Formerly under Japanese control, the Truk Islands became a U.S. Trusteeship after World War II, and the government agency that sponsored the research was the U.S. Navy.

bone in front (A), the bones from the hips at either side (B), and the coccyx (C),* i.e., the lower spine in back. This diamond could very well be characterized as a "gate of jewels," for beyond its threshold lie layer upon layer of parts that make the vagina an entity "full of things."

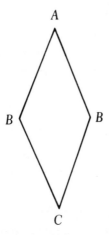

A

B   B

C

Fig. 32 Schematic Diagram of "The Gate of Jewels"

In passion, the vagina, far from being a passive space, is a complex entity of active space and deeper-lying sexual parts. Since it is an entity, what affects one part also affects the others. These reciprocal responses include five specific actions that enhance female orgasmic response: the "surge" or erection of the vagina, the "bearing down" from the upper vagina, and the "clasping," "caressing," "kissing," actions of the middle and lower vagina.

Most of the names we use for body parts were first introduced by Greek physicians. Vulva is today

*Coccyx, which in Greek literally means "cuckoo," was so named because this small triangular bone at the base of the spine was thought to resemble the shape of a cuckoo's bill.

a comprehensive name for the external genital organs of the female, which, according to Webster's New World Dictionary (1956), include "the labia majora, labia minora, clitoris and the entrance to the vagina." In Latin, the name means "wrapper" or "covering," presumably a reference to the surface skin that "wraps" the outer genitals.* In naming the sexual parts of women, metaphors were often taken from the more familiar parts of the human body, like the crura of the clitoris, which means the "legs."

The metaphor anatomists used for naming the female genital folds was the lips of the mouth; they called the large fleshy outer folds "the greater lips" (the labia majora) and the smaller slender inner folds "the little lips" (the labia minora). From close perspective, when the greater lips are parted, wing-like, the little lips become visible. Above the little lips rests the Lowndes crown covered by a half-fold.

*H. D. Jocelyn, a Latinist, and B. P. Setchell, a biologist, have annotated their translation of Regnier de Graaf's 1672 treatise on the generative organs of women with many helpful explanations of usage of early anatomical terms, among them an etymological note that "*vulva* was applied normally to the uterus, vagina and vestibule, regarded as one entity, and only occasionally just to the vagina and its vestibule." They note also that much earlier "a *vulva* was strictly the uterus of an animal" before Celsus (53 B.C.–A.D. 7) "extended the usage of *vulva* to the human uterus (2.7.10 and elsewhere)." Usage was confused and continues to be confusing to the modern reader. As an example, de Graaf himself writes in his treatise that the part is called the vulva "from *valvae,* 'folding doors,' or, as some think, from *velle,* 'want,' on the grounds that it has a great and insatiable want of coitus." But the experts Jocelyn and Setchell tell us that this etymology is plainly absurd and that de Graaf should not have mentioned it.

I have not come across any explanation of exactly how the meaning of vulva came to be transferred from the human uterus to the outer genitals.

When both the greater and the little lips are parted, another surface, called the vestibule, comes into view. If the half-fold is then drawn back to expose the Lowndes crown, one can observe that:

1. The inner sides of the little lips have the same bright pink color as the Lowndes crown. (These colorations, of course, vary somewhat, depending upon a woman's basic pigmentation.)

2. The two little lips do not actually join each other. Instead, they come pinpoint close and insert themselves into the crown (Figure 33). Their edges are slightly corrugated just before joining the crown, so that in elevation a number of tiny scalloped curves can be observed (Figure 33).

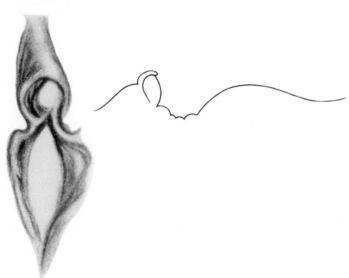

FIG. 33 Labia Minora and Crown: viewed frontally (*Adapted from Dickinson, 1949*) and in lateral schematic elevation

Although these forwardmost attachments are actually double, they are usually referred to in the singular as the frenulum, a word which originally meant "the corner of the mouth where the lips join."

In most women, this juncture of the little lips and the Lowndes crown is extremely responsive to erotic stimulation. The counterpart in the male—a true single frenulum—arises from the foreskin as a very thin longitudinal fold (left intact in circumcised men) that is attached to the glans on its urethral (ventral) side. Similarly, as an area close to the Lowndes crown, it is extremely sensitive to sexual stimulation.

In repose, the greater lips lie close together and form two cushion-like folds over the genitals. Unlike the greater, the little lips do not contain any fat cells, but they are "soft" in a different way—their surfaces, especially the inner sides, are as soft to the touch as the inside of the mouth.

Both structures vary considerably in size from woman to woman and may undergo some natural change in the same woman from adolescence to middle age. On the average, the little lips in their "resting" state may project as little as three eighths of an inch and be not much more than an inch and a quarter long, with a thickness of about one eighth of an inch.

Generally, the fullest projection of the little lips is found adjacent to the woman's glans, from which point they gradually taper down lengthwise to an indistinct vanishing point in the flesh of the greater lips near the vaginal opening. Rarely do they project beyond the greater lips. Some incidences of greatly extended projections have been reported as natural

FIG. 34 The Hottentot Venus, Saartjie Baartman: an
early nineteenth-century drawing

growths among American and European women,
and among the Hottentots, elongation of the little lips
is purposely manipulated (Figure 34).*

The Trukese women also encourage some projection of the little lips, but their aesthetic preference
is for adornment rather than aggrandizement. They
perforate the labia (presumably the little lips) and

*J. L. Moreau, *Histoire de la femme* (Paris, 1803).

insert dangling ornaments that tinkle as they walk proudly with legs slightly apart.

The Trukese include the visible outer female genitalia as part of the vagina; the Japanese focus on the "genital jewels" inside the vagina. In the West, the vagina is thought of only as the internal organ beyond the entrance.

The confusion of the anatomists before Fallopio stemmed from their inability to perceive a distinction between substance (the cervix) and space (the passageway). Fallopio recognized the space and its correct relationship to the substance in question (i.e., the cervix). But the anatomists left things at that, making no attempt to relate the passageway to the real substance of the vagina. In the following sections, a new perspective on the vagina as both active space and amorous substance will be presented. But first let us consider the shape, angle, and size of the space.

Variously described as a tube, a barrel, and a canal, the vagina is actually more complex in its overall shape than these terms suggest. Viewed from the side, the roof of the vagina bulges inward and then dips back, continuing in a downward curve toward the apex where it surrounds the cervix. The floor of the vagina follows the same curve, at rest, but without a similar bulging and dipping (Figure 35). Viewed from the front, if one could see with X-ray vision, the vagina is cone-shaped (Figure 36). The lower fourth (A) is the narrow part at the bottom of the cone. The middle is the broadest part, and narrows at the top just enough to encircle the cervix.

The vagina's space is often depicted in cross section as being in the form of an "H" (Figure 37). But

FIG. 35 Side View of the Vagina: a similar configuration
is shown in Fig. 22; shaded area in inset outlines contour
of bulge into ceiling of vagina

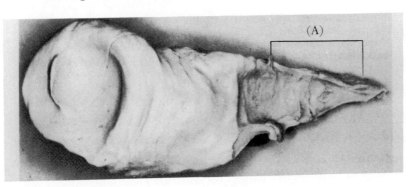

FIG. 36 Frontal View of the Vagina: (A) indicates lower
fourth

this is the shape of the middle length only. The more
muscular lower vagina does not assume the "H"
form unless a woman is under anesthesia or unless
all her muscles are in a comparable state of utter
relaxation. Otherwise, even when the vagina appears to be in the "resting state," the muscles are

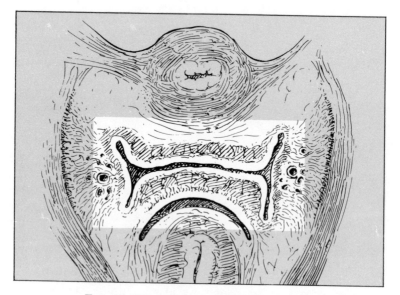

FIG. 37 Cross Section of the Mid-vagina

under a certain tension and kept at the ready. This muscular tension, which controls the shape of the lower vagina, makes the opening appear slightly rounded, not H-shaped.

The passageway is capable, within certain limits, of adapting itself to the shape of the object introduced into it. By its nature, the vagina responds immediately to displacement, then its substance makes it tend to "hug." Its double yielding/constricting nature comes from the fact that the space is highly expandable but controlled by a number of very effective muscles. The shape of the passageway is not determined by displacement alone. During stimulation, it is actively altered by the swelling of the various vaginal parts that make up its substance and by the actions of the muscles at each level.

The angles of the passageway at different levels

were extensively studied by the gynecologist Robert Latou Dickinson, who made some interesting observations in his *Human Sex Anatomy.* By describing an imaginary line between the pubic bone in front and the coccyx at the base of the spine, he determined the basic "tilt" of a woman's whole pelvic area (Figure 38). Then the angles of the passageway could be determined in relation to that vertical line. The angle near the opening proved to be very different from that in the middle. About an inch or so inside the entrance, a change of direction occurred, so that the upper three fourths lay in a more horizontal position (Figure 39). As the vagina actively responds to stimulation, the angle of the passageway alters and becomes very similar to the angle of the erect penis in the conventional coital position (Figures 40, 41).

FIG. 38 "Tilt" of the Female Pelvic Area

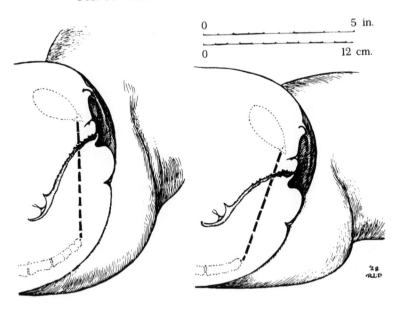

In the average adult woman, the length of the vaginal space is about four inches. The roof is shortened by the projection of the cervix into its length by a half inch or more, making the floor correspondingly longer.

As shown in Figure 36, the vaginal space is different in width at different levels. During stimulation, these various widths do not remain constant; each constricts and dilates depending upon the degree of sexual stimulation and the woman's response thereto.

At the entrance to the vagina, in the flare of the trumpet-shaped vestibule, the only visible part is the glans. Immediately below is the slightly rounded recess of the vaginal opening.

The edge of the woman's glans (called the carina) defines the beginning of the roof of the vagina. Just beyond the carina one can feel the bulge that, according to the new theory, contains the female spongiosum and prostatic glands. As we have seen, this bulge extends for an inch or more and is a

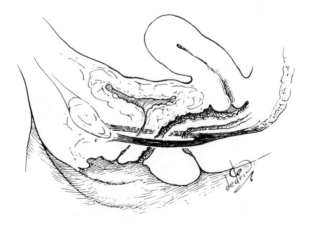

Fig. 39 Horizontal Position of the Upper Vagina

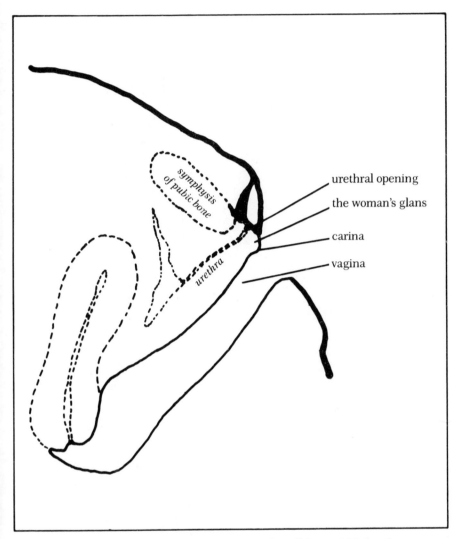

FIG. 40 Angle of Vagina in Stimulated State (*Adapted from Dickinson, 1949*)

site of intense sensitivity. The surface of the area is composed of tiny ridges and furrows called rugae (Latin for "folds"), which are most pronounced in the groovelike spaces to either side of the bulge and may extend to the floor of the lower vagina but tend to

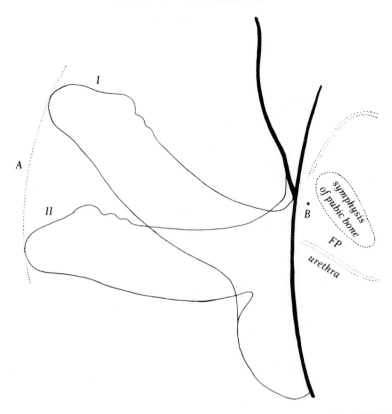

FIG. 41 Angle of Penis in Stimulated State (I) and Angle of Deflection During Coitus (II): angle I is average obtained by continuing the axis of the fixed portion (FP) outward based on 16 anatomical sections; A to B equals length of penis (*Above figure is shown at two thirds the size of original Dickinson illustration drawn of male in standing position*)

smooth out in the middle and upper sections. They make an uneven surface that, during coitus, creates very pleasurable gripping and rubbing sensations in the lower vagina and awareness of increased friction against the penis, all of which is equally pleasurable to the man.

In the narrow spaces to either side of the vagina there is a vast network of arteries that brings blood from the heart to the sexual parts, and an equally rich network of veins that carries it back.

In addition, supporting ligaments hold the suspended vagina and genitals in place, and muscles that run along the length of the vagina mingle with the muscles that surround the vagina. These both play an important role in the sexual responses of women and will be described in detail in a later section.

The surface area between the thighs that makes up the space between the vagina and the anus is called the perineum. In the male, it is defined by the area between the base of the penis and the anus. The

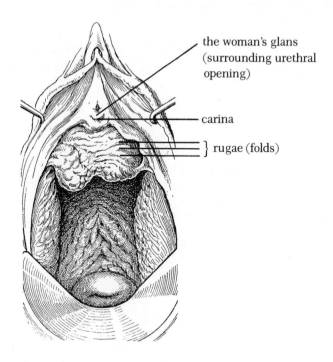

the woman's glans (surrounding urethral opening)

carina

} rugae (folds)

FIG. 42 Open Vagina with Rugae (Folds) Exposed

word comes from a Greek word meaning "to swim around" something and is used for the perineum because it usually is moist with perspiration. In some of the medical writings of the ancient Greeks, the female perineum was referred to as the "ejaculatory muscle," a term that suggests that a sexual function was attributed to it.

When physicians use the term today, they often mean all the structures that fill up the area below the pelvic diaphragm. (These are listed in Appendix B.) One of them is the highly excitable perineal body located in the floor of the vagina.

The floor of the vagina and the anus are in very close relationship to each other, but between them in the lower vagina is the interposing perineal body, "PB" for short (Figure 43). A small muscular mass shaped like a pyramid, the PB is anchored to the body structure. Its broad base runs between the vaginal and anal openings at the surface and extends back

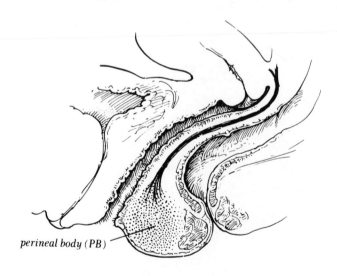

perineal body (PB)

FIG. 43 Female Perineal Body

for about an inch. In the male, the PB is about half an inch wide, up to three quarters of an inch crosswise, and located close to the urethra, between the prostate and the bulb (Figure 44). The width of the female PB varies considerably from individual to individual but is always wider and thicker than the male.

Leonardo da Vinci believed that the presence of sphincter muscles around openings in the body could be determined by a certain puckering or wrinkling of the skin which occurs if the muscles are large at one end and narrow at the other, that is, pyramidal in shape. He did some sketches based on the idea—which he himself recognized was only tentative—that such muscles around the anus are arranged in a circular petal-like formation (Figure 45). Unusual as it may seem, consensus has yet to be reached among scientists on the precise anatomy of the PB. Physicians do agree, however, that the PB is a center

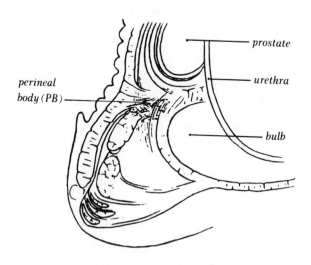

FIG. 44 Male Perineal Body

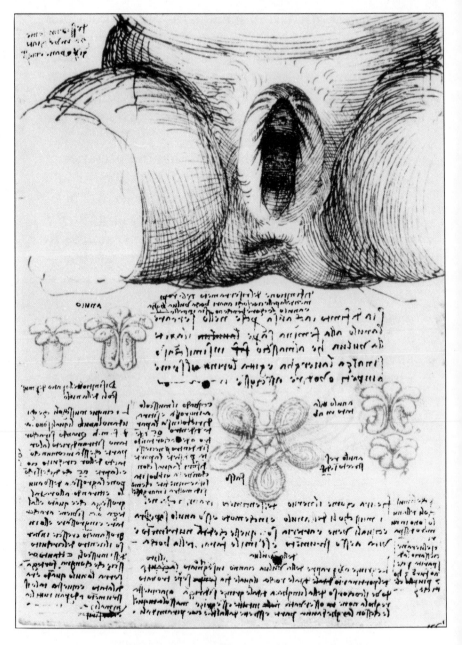

FIG. 45 The Female Anatomy: muscles around the anus
(*da Vinci*, Quaderni d'Anatomie *III, 1511–1516*)

of much activity and use expressions like "a heavily used traffic center" or "a central hub" to describe its function in a complex of crisscrossing muscles.*

Any tactile stimulation of the PB or pressure upon it creates erotic arousal, assuming desire is present. As a result of sexual stimulation of the PB, the rear lower vagina puffs out and, acting reciprocally with penile pressure, intensifies erotic sensation for both partners.

The other end of the floor of the vagina, at its apex, joins the cervix, creating an archlike area that is more spacious than the opposite arch in front of the cervix already described. During the deep thrusting of coitus, the rear arch receives the penis.

This recessed area has been known to tear during coitus. It almost never happens, and when it does, it is usually because a couple is experiencing coitus for the first time, or for the first time in a long period. The reason why the injury is so uncommon is that the vagina is usually accommodating to the penis, and, if it is not, the highly refined sensors in the penile glans act as a safeguarding signal to the experienced male.

Some women report that even slight pressure in the archlike space during coitus causes sensations that are among the most intensely pleasurable that they experience. Why this should be true physiologically is not yet clear. One can only guess that sexual stimulation of the area may cause a spreading of pleasurable sensation because the arch is very close to the sacral nerves and, theoretically, any stimula-

*These last muscles, which are listed in Appendix B, are described in the next section.

tion of the area could induce stimulation of these nerves.

Leonardo's interest in the musculature surrounding the openings in the body included an interest in the lower vaginal musculature, which he called "the gatekeeper of the castle." By self-admission, Leonardo's knowledge of the detailed anatomy of these muscles remained cloudy. In describing the same muscles four hundred years later in 1949, Dickinson affirmed that there are no other muscles in the human body about which such nebulous impressions prevail, or whose form and function are so difficult to understand. It is very hard to visualize the complex form of these muscles, but their function is somewhat better understood today.

There are three groups of muscles in the deeper structures of the vagina. In ascending order, they are the muscles found in the perineal body, the urogenital diaphragm, and the pelvic diaphragm (see Appendix B). These muscles are highly responsive to sexual stimulation; when kindled into action by the nervous system, they cause an increased amount of blood to flow into the sexual organs and bring about general overall swelling of the genital area. Each of these groups plays a part in female erection, in the building up of excitement, and in the clasping/caressing/kissing actions that lead to orgasm.

The first two groups—those in the PB and the urogenital diaphragm—are both considered part of the perineum. At this "gatekeeper" level, there are in addition to muscles that support the vagina from side to side and muscles that constrict the urethra and anus, muscles that cover the crura of the clitoris and one that covers the bulbs.

In my description of the female bulbs, I mentioned the fact that upon stimulation they become swollen. When the covering bulbo-spongiosum muscle is stimulated, it contracts and makes the vagina tighter. The muscle can constrict the passageway because, in addition to covering the bulbs, the bulbo-spongiosum loops around and surrounds the vaginal opening.

By its action, the bulbo-spongiosum also pushes the swollen, rounded bulbs up and inward. In this position, the bulbs may be observed behind the carina to either side of the woman's glans. The left bulb is usually more prominent than the right. Dickinson made this same observation, explaining that since "the left bulb is usually structurally larger than the other, one-sided protrusion is not uncommon."* It does not indicate that the left side is any more erotically excitable than the right.

In their swollen, repositioned state, the mass of both bulbs makes the opening of the vagina smaller. The consequent increase in genital friction in this area, combined with the tightening of the vaginal opening, contributes to the "clasping" action of the vagina. This intensifies the sense of genital closeness for both partners. When the bulbs are in their puffed, more exposed state, they themselves are highly sensitive to gentle tactile stimulation, and during coitus they are also sensitive to pressure from the penis.

With the repositioning of the bulbs, the roof of the vagina, containing the spongiosum and prostatic glands, moves forward to where it can exert a "caressing" action during coitus. In certain positions,

*Robert Latou Dickinson, *Human Sex Anatomy* (Baltimore: Williams & Wilkins Company, 1949), p. 49.

the vaginal caress is felt by the man as a subtle undulation from the roof of the vagina against the penis that is most clearly discerned through its massaging effect on the glans. The reciprocal actions of penile stroking and vaginal caressing evoke a strong response in the woman and an increased flow of sexual fluids. In both sexes, the sensations induced by the combined mutual caressing/massaging actions during coitus, together with other impulses from the entire urogenital area, are transmitted to the spinal cord via the pudendal nerve and sacral plexus and then on to the brain to bring about orgasm.

At a certain stage of stimulation, the muscles covering the crura of the clitoris contract and by this shortening action pull on the Lowndes crown, thereby moving it even closer to the vagina. These muscles are hidden, as are the crura themselves, but one observable demonstration of their activity is this retraction of the crown.

As the woman's excitement grows, the lower vagina is contracted involuntarily during the orgasmic "takeover." But by concentrating, women are also capable of effecting a rhythmic "squeezing" of the muscles in the lower vagina, which action tightens the opening. By exerting this voluntary action during coitus, the woman may enjoy a highly erotic sense of "kissing" the penis, which action also draws the little lips together. The man perceives the "kissing" action as a titillating, intermittent compression around the penis.

The third group of muscles—those that are part of the pelvic diaphragm—includes one of the principal players in the scenario of the sexual act. It is known technically by the formidable name of pubococcygeus, which I will call for short the pc. This muscle rings the middle vagina, beginning about an inch or so inside the opening. The pc originates at the pubic bone as two bands about half an inch on each side from the center. These form an oval ring that very closely surrounds the urethra, vagina, PB, and rectum (Figure 46).

The right and left bands come together at the coccyx, the bottom of the spine, where their "bellies" fuse together to form a horizontal plate that supports the vagina, the uterus, and the rectum.

When the pc responds to sexual stimulation, it moves in from the rear toward the vagina—the action that makes the vagina surge forward. This dramatic surge is what makes the vagina "straighten out." It is, in effect, another kind of female erection. By this change of angle, the vagina becomes even more accommodating and receptive to the erect penis. The general axis of the erect vagina and the angle of the erect penis are about the same, as shown

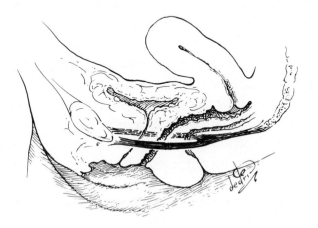

FIG. 46 The Pubococcygeus or "PC" Muscle (*The illustration used for the above figure appears earlier in this chapter as Fig. 39*)

in earlier illustrations. At the same time, the pc "squeezes" the vagina from side to side, which once more enhances the pleasure for both the man and the woman, because of the squeezing sensation itself and the generally increased friction.

The pc muscle acts in coordination with the muscles in the abdomen. Contract or relax the abdominal muscles, and the pc will reciprocate. The pc is brought into play in this way when a woman reaches a certain stage of sexual excitement and begins to "bear down."

For some women, the bearing-down action is very significant in achieving orgasm. Dickinson reports a case study of a thirty-seven-year-old married woman, mother of two children, who could induce orgasm by this means alone. She would set her chest muscles, fix the muscles in her abdomen, and bear down twice a second with pauses, sometimes for a total of up to eighty-three thrusts. This process is the same basic action described above, which brings into play the reciprocal action of the pc. According to Dickinson, it causes the roof of the vagina to move back and forth (Figure 47), producing the caressing motion. While a woman has voluntary control of the bearing down, the caressing action occurs without a conscious effort to make it happen. It results from the physical repositioning of the bulging area in the roof of the vagina, a change of position that Dickinson notes in his illustration as a moving forward of the anterior vaginal wall.

Dickinson also describes the descent of the uterus as part of this kind of sexual response in women. When a woman bears down, the action exerts pressure on the uterus, which in turn makes the

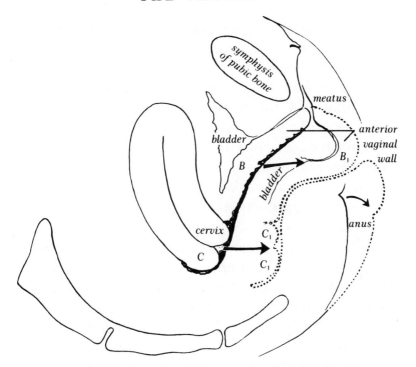

FIG. 47 Range of Vaginal Displacement When Orgasm Is Induced by Violent, Rhythmic Straining with Descent of the Uterus; anterior vaginal wall moves forward 1 inch, indicated by dotted line (*Dickinson, 1949*)

cervix move about an inch into the vagina and, during coitus, a rhythmic back-and-forth action is set in motion.

The descent of the uterus during sexual arousal is also mentioned by Kinsey, who states: "Strong rhythmic contractions of the abdominal muscles sometimes push the uterus and the attached walls of the vagina closer to the vaginal entrance if it is not blocked by the inserted penis."* This is not to say that the bearing-down action does not occur if the penis

*Kinsey, et al., *op. cit.*, p. 633.

is in the vagina. In fact, the presence of the penis as something to push against facilitates the action. But neither the uterus nor the penis is essential. Women who have had their uteruses surgically removed report that they still experience the bearing-down response; and with or without the uterus present, the response may be elicited by sexual stimulation that does not require the presence of the penis in the vagina.

Kinsey does not include the uterus among the organs involved in sexual response, nor does he consider the cervix to be a source of erotic stimulation. He specifically mentions that "all of the clinical and experimental data show that the surface of the cervix is the most completely insensitive part of the female genital anatomy."* It should be noted, however, that Kinsey does report an increase in the size of the uterus during sexual stimulation. The finding is corroborated by Masters and Johnson, who go on to explain that Kinsey's original data were obtained from periodic pelvic examinations of a prostitute during a full work period (five and a half hours) and six hours thereafter.†

Surgical removal of the uterus has reached such epidemic proportions in the United States that the practice has become an issue of concern both outside and within the medical profession. Opinions differ widely as to the importance of the uterus to a woman's overall sexuality. And, as I have said, many women who have had hysterectomies do not seem to notice any change in their sexual response or in

*Kinsey, et al., *op. cit.*, p. 584.
†William H. Masters and Virginia E. Johnson, *Human Sexual Response* (Boston: Little, Brown, 1966), pp. 119–122.

reaching orgasm. Other women, however, do note a change. Some physicians advise their patients that removal of the uterus will not affect their sexual response in any way and that their male partners will never even notice the difference. Other physicians are reluctant to perform a hysterectomy unless absolutely necessary; when they do, they feel compelled to advise their patients that the surgery may result in some change in sexual response.

The term "uterus" was originally intended to apply only to the womb in its water-filled, pregnant state. The literal meaning of the word is "a leather water bag." It is thought that the name was introduced as early as the first century B.C.—a time when animal-skin bags were familiar everyday objects. Now, of course, "uterus" is used whether or not the organ contains new life. The primary function of the organ is a reproductive one. But, as we have seen, the cervix is capable of quite a bit of upward movement during coitus. The impact of the penis can displace the cervix upward as much as an inch or two and create a certain amount of "uterine jostling."

In antiquity, the uterus was actually thought to be capable of wandering inside a woman's body with or without help from a man's penis. This notion of a "wandering uterus" goes back to Plato and was described in the fourth century B.C. by the "father of medicine," Hippocrates, who believed that when the uterus became dry, it wandered around inside a woman's body in search of moisture. Up until the seventeenth century, it was still generally believed that the uterus could rise into a woman's throat, and that such displacement was the cause of fits of hysteria, the symptoms of which included weariness, palpitations of the heart, weak pulse, dizziness, and others. For almost two thousand years, the concept that hysteria in women was caused by a "wandering uterus" held sway. Then, in 1616, one man's simple but cogent thought on the notion reduced it to nonsense. A physician named Charles Lepois (1563–1633) contended that since men as well as women suffered the very same symptoms, the uterus could not possibly be the cause, but rather that in both sexes the cause of such attacks could be linked with the brain and neural system.

In the matter of the "wandering uterus," the only voice heard was that of the male; women were unheeded. In the matter of vaginal pleasure, a contemporary subject that also intimately touches their lives, the voices of women again, until recently, have gone unheard. Medical opinion has been opposed to the idea that the vagina is an organ of any significant sexual sensitivity, and doctors today continue to underestimate the erotic character of the vagina.

Despite seemingly authoritative reports of the vagina's insensitivity offered by medical researchers, women themselves do not universally share the medical point of view—a fact that the sexual partners of these women can attest to.

In *The Second Sex,* Simone de Beauvoir wrote about vaginal pleasure, and in so doing tried to express something that most women know to be a fact of life. A few other women have also tried to have the positive side of the issue heard, but to no avail. In the last few decades, though there has been increasing cultural interest in the nature of the female sexual response, the emphasis in medicine and among the lay public alike has been on the clitoris, not the vagina, as the primary female sexual organ.

There can be no denying that the knowledge gained about the clitoris in this process has helped both men and women to better understand the female sexual response. Knowledge about the clitoris is important, as is knowledge about the vagina. But to think of one of these parts as separate from the other or of paramount importance in the female sexual response is to lose perspective on the complexity of that response. The theory presented here proposes that the clitoris, the urethra, and the vagina function as a unit.

The scientific method necessarily isolates elements in order to study the way in which the parts compose the whole. In the case of sexuality, this does not mean a focus on the genitals alone; it is equally important to remember that orgasm involves the brain and consciousness as well. At times, however, the body is capable of a spontaneous expression of feelings that a man or woman might find difficult to verbalize.

In *A Lover's Discourse,* Roland Barthes writes, "What I hide by my language, my body utters."* The point of Barthes's observation is that the formal language we use often tends to obscure things, whereas the sensual language of lovers tends to reveal them. And it reveals them through a vocabulary of signs —of movement or sounds or a certain "look" in the eyes—signs which are subtle but universally understood. Without these signs, most men and women would feel at a loss to express what they feel. Formal language has an extremely limited sexual vocabu-

*Roland Barthes, *A Lover's Discourse* (New York: Hill and Wang, 1978), p. 44.

lary; by design, it has focused on the reproductive function, which it separates from the sexual function. For this reason, most of the language used in relation to the vagina is concerned with the fact that it is through the vagina that women menstruate, get pregnant, and give birth.

The sensual language of lovers also tends to separate the functions of reproduction and sex. Except for the relatively short period of child-producing years, the emphasis of their language is on *sexual* function; and it very decidedly does not neglect the vagina as a sexual organ.

Kinsey's work had great appeal to couples, because here was a scientist willing for the first time to emphasize the sexual aspects of reproduction. Furthermore, he was among the first to try to convince men and women that in terms of *sexual* function the two sexes are identical. In *Sexual Behavior in the Human Female,* he concludes: "In spite of the widespread and oft-repeated emphasis on the supposed differences between female and male sexuality, we fail to find any anatomic or physiological basis for such difference."*

In the Kinsey tradition, contemporary research places emphasis on sexual function. Scientists today also follow Kinsey and a long tradition in accepting without question certain "givens" about the female anatomy and about male/female counterparts. What specifically does Kinsey say about the idea of a male counterpart to the vagina? As a thoroughgoing scientist noted for his precision, Kinsey himself does consider the idea. But it is only in passing that he states

*Kinsey, et al., *op. cit.,* p. 641.

the following opinion in the matter: "There is no functional homologue of the vagina in the male."*

This statement appears on the surface to be inconsistent with Kinsey's basic premise that in terms of sexual function there is no difference between the sexes. If one proceeds from the assumption that Kinsey *is* being consistent, there are other ways to interpret this statement. He could be basing his conclusion on a positive matching of negative findings, i.e.: the female vagina is not a center of eroticism; no anatomical basis exists in the male for "vaginal" eroticism; therefore, in terms of sexual function, men and women are still alike. In other words, what the female doesn't enjoy, the male doesn't enjoy either. On the other hand, it could be that Kinsey was uncharacteristically reverting to a reference to *reproductive* function. Of course, if one thinks of the vagina from such a perspective, which views the organ as a relatively insensitive hollow with nothing in it except a surface lining, the idea of a male counterpart does not appear to be a likely proposition, or even one worth considering.

The clarification of the relevant male and female counterparts, interesting as a subject in itself, is also a matter of basic importance, for it is a means of clarifying sexual function. In this light, the idea that a counterpart of the vagina exists in the male is worth pursuing. From the new perspective of the vagina as an entity composed of a number of sexually

*Ibid., p. 580. Kinsey, trained as a biologist, brought to the field of research on human sexuality an attitude of precision developed while working in the Radcliffe Zoology Laboratory on painstaking anatomical measurements of gallwasps.

responsive parts, the proposition is not that unlikely. The parts that, together with the vaginal muscles, contribute in a fundamental way to erotic response are: the glans and its carina, the spongiosum and bulbs, and the clitoral crown, corpus, and crura. Below is a schematic three-dimensional model of the substance of the vagina (Figure 48). This new perspective of the vagina is so different from the old one that it would seem in order to give the entity a new name. Instead, I prefer to keep the name "vagina," but to change its meaning.

As a way of visualizing the new perspective of the vagina, begin by thinking of the formation of the Lowndes crown and the little lips on the surface. They look like the letter "Y" inverted, or a lambda shape. This lambda shape is paralleled inside by the

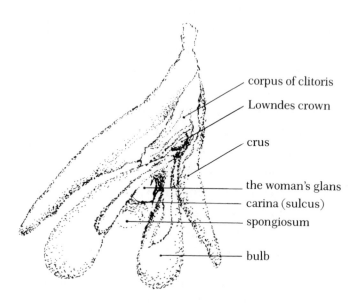

corpus of clitoris
Lowndes crown
crus
the woman's glans
carina (sulcus)
spongiosum
bulb

FIG. 48 Three-Dimensional Model of the Substance of the Vagina

crura of the clitoris and the bulbs as extensions of the crown and the glans. The vaginal structure can be likened to that of a tree; only the crown and the glans are visible to the eye, whereas the remaining nine tenths of its substance is hidden below the surface. Another analogy that suggests itself—the iceberg— would be unfitting for two reasons: its obvious conno- tation of coldness, and the fact that the vagina is securely attached to the surrounding bony structure, whereas an iceberg floats.

The lambda shapes are superimposed one be- hind the other in three layers: outer layer—the little lips; middle layer—the bulbs; and inner layer—the legs. As shown in Figure 49, each of the structures present in the vagina is present in the penis: the glans and sulcus, the spongiosum and bulb, and the clitoral crown, corpus and crura. Furthermore, each of the functional systems linked to the genital area in the human body—the nerves, the blood vessels, as well as the muscles—is similar in the two sexes. Since the anatomical bases for arousal and orgasm that make the vagina function as an entity also exist in the male, it does not seem reasonable to single out the vagina as an exception in the theory of sexual counterparts. In fact, the traditional theory of ana- tomical counterparts contends that the male does have a structure homologous to the vagina, but that the part in question is only vestigial in form. The vestige, called the vagina masculina, or the prostatic utricle, is located between the male ejaculatory ducts.* A little tubelike finger, it projects from the

---

*This same evagination is at times referred to as the *utriculus masculinus* by some scientists who claim that it is as

rear wall of the urethra into the prostate. I propose instead that the true male counterpart of the vagina is the penis.

Galen's idea of the vagina as "a penis turned inside out" immediately returns to mind. Is Galen "the wonder worker" to be vindicated after all? The vagina may not actually be "a penis turned inside out"—nothing as simple as that—but, in my opinion, Galen's insight concerning the vagina and penis as counterparts was not incorrect but merely incomplete.

At the outset of the scientific study of sexual parts, it was the male anatomy that was identified and named first; the female anatomy was then identified in relation to what was known about the male. Since all the parts of the penis exist in close proximity to one another within one unified structure, the traditional anatomists could not help but perceive the penis as an entity. From a perception of this unity, the orderly process of identification of the individual parts followed—always with a sense of their basic interrelationship and sexual function. In the female anatomy, no such overall unifying structure is as conspicuous, nor are the sexual parts as closely organized as in the penis. The anatomists could not easily perceive the vagina as an entity of interrelated parts. As a result, they identified the female parts in isolation from one another in a reductionist manner, which made it difficult to perceive the coordinated function of these parts.

---

well a vestige of the uterus. Deter, Caldwell, and Folsom, *op. cit.,* explain that "the name *utriculus masculinus* is used to show that this gland is homologous with the uterus of the female"—p. 653.

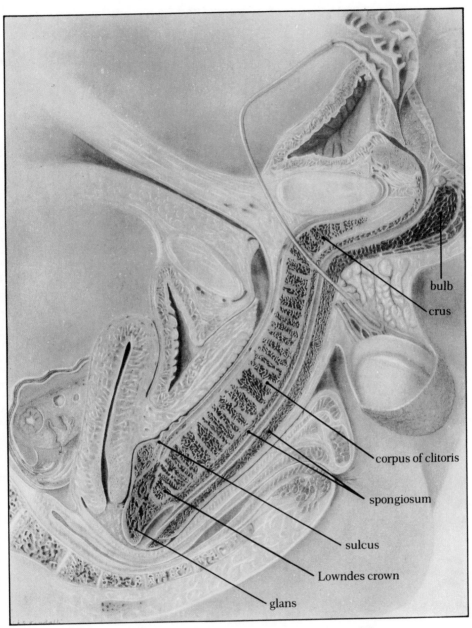

F<small>IG</small>. 49 Male and Female Sexual Organs in Coital Position (*Adapted from Dickinson, 1949*)

Once the vagina is perceived as an entity of sexual parts, in the way that the penis has always been perceived, it becomes clear that the true counterparts are not the penis and clitoris, nor are they the prostatic utricle and the vagina; the true counterparts are the penis and the vagina.

CHAPTER 5

The Physiology of Passion

Eyes see; ears hear. Each part of our bodies has a specific role. There are moments, however, when men and women can be metaphysical about the senses—their own and each other's. Through the senses, in passion, we transcend the senses and reach a point when, to adapt a phrase from Martin Buber, we can taste pleasure with our eyes. But is this true in the same way and to the same degree for both of us? "Do you feel what I feel?" the man asks the woman, the woman asks the man.

If a couple turns to the experts for an answer, they will find that current theory claims that the state of readiness for coitus, for example, is signaled by different phenomena in the male and in the female. The male sign is the rigid penis, the female, the show of vaginal "lubrication"—the experts' term for genital wetness. The trouble with this idea is that the criterion for female "readiness" is based on a consideration of "readiness" from a male point of view. Some women feel very ready for coitus without any expression of sexual fluid. Others even prefer to have such expression elicited by a gentle preliminary stroking of the vagina by the penis. If the vagina causes too much friction against the penis, the man has any number of alternatives for moistening it, such as kissing.

The real error is to equate male erection with the expression of female sexual fluid as representative of the same stage of genital excitation. When the man's penis becomes erect, he is pre-orgasmic but anatomically "primed" for orgasm. The comparable state of readiness for orgasm in women is, according to the new theory, the simultaneous response of the clitoris, the urethra, the vagina, and their related structures, which I call the C.U.V. response.

By looking at the female anatomy in the unstimulated "resting" state, one can observe the locations of the female Lowndes crown and the woman's glans. These highly erogenous female parts may be no more than three quarters of an inch apart,* but apart they are. In the "resting" anatomy, the adult female sexual parts are individually complex; in passion, they become an even more complex unity. In arousal there is an increased flow of blood to these parts. I suggest that in the process of swelling and expansion that takes place, the C.U.V. parts transform themselves into a functional unit. It already has been noted that after a certain amount of stimulation, the clitoral tip retracts. But rather than becoming "buried," as some authorities think is the case, it

*Two cm from base of the Lowndes crown to the top (that is, the closest point) of the urethral opening in the woman's glans.

may be positioning itself in closer proximity to the other parts of the C.U.V. unit as part of the same transforming process.

As we have seen, in the adult male the Lowndes crown is tucked under the penile glans, putting these extremely sensitive sexual parts in the closest possible proximity to each other. Touch or press upon the glans, especially its ridge (the sulcus), and you excite the Lowndes crown as well.

When the C.U.V. response has been elicited, a woman experiences heightened sensitivity. At this stage, the C.U.V. structures become a unified sensory organ, through which a woman perceives sensations of touch and pressure—both active (that is, she senses what it touches and presses against) and receptive (she senses it being touched and any pressure upon it). Like the erect penile unit, this female organ of unified parts is primed for orgasm.

In pointing up the difference in the organization of male/female sexual parts, the new theory suggests possible explanations for one of the much-talked-about differences between the sexes—the timing of sexual response. Scientific observation has established that the woman *can* respond as quickly as the man. In practice, however, many men and women still observe that the woman is usually slower. Thus, during coitus, the male tries to delay his responses, and the female—appreciative of the fact that the man could achieve orgasm soon after coitus begins —is aware that if she delays her own too long, she may be left in a state of sexual suspension. The traditional explanation for the more rapid sexual responses of the male focuses on the differences between the psychological makeup of the man and the woman. Kinsey sums up the difference in his statement that more males than females are psychologically conditioned to consider the genitalia as *the* structures primarily associated with sexual response, that males attach much more importance to the genitalia than females do in a sexual relationship. The assumption is that a woman tends actually to downplay the importance of the genitals and that her psychological need is to believe that she as a total person is attractive to the male. Identification of the C.U.V. response in women provides a much more plausible basis and is more consistent with earlier scientific observation of the natural speed of sexual responses in the female. In terms of sequence, erection and the C.U.V. response occur before the onset of orgasmic contractions.

The Lowndes crowns theory has shown that the female crown is clearly visible and directly touchable, whereas the male crown is inside the penis and always covered. Knowledge of this fact suggests a possible reason why women usually take longer than men to have an orgasm. Van de Velde reminds us of the well-known medical fact that "the exposed male glans takes longer to reach the summit of stimulation than the covered."* It is for this reason anthropologists suggest that in so many cultures around the world men are circumcised, the purpose of which is the prolongation of coitus.† Van de Velde accepts as obvious that such prolongation is highly

*Van de Velde, *op. cit.,* p. 200.
†Ibid., p. 200. See Fehlinger, cited by Van de Velde, *Sexual Life of Primitive Peoples* (Leipzig: K. Kabitzsch, 1921).

favorable to the majority of women, but he finds it difficult to determine "whether the lessened susceptibility of the glans means diminished sexual enjoyment on the man's side, or whether his enjoyment is increased through the prolongation of the act." Van de Velde cites an interesting anthropological account, which corroborates that in circumcised males the more exposed male glans becomes desensitized:

> The "native" boys, who collect together in the stations and plantations, discuss sexual matters among themselves, and it is well known that those who are circumcised have much less tactile sensibility in the glans than those who are not. The circumcised men admit frankly that they take longer before ejaculation than their fellows.*

On the basis of these observations, one might reasonably expect that because the female crown is exposed, it would have to be stimulated for a longer period of time than the covered male crown in order to achieve a comparable sexual response.

Others who have compared the nerve endings in these parts of the anatomy report that because of the high density of sensory-nerve endings in the female clitoral tip, it is far more sensitive than the male glans; but prolonged stimulation in the exact same spot of either the male glans or the female clitoral tip can cause a numbing effect.

Altogether, these findings provide a basis for proposing that, following the C.U.V.-response/erect-

*Van de Velde, *op. cit.,* pp. 199–200. Frederici, *Contributions to Anthropology and Philology of German New Guinea* (Berlin: Documents about German Protectorates, Spl. 5, 1912).

penis stage, both a woman and a man experience the same sequence of sexual sensations:

1. Contractions

2. Orgasm

3. Ejaculation

4. Deflation

The findings of others concerning contractions are probably familiar to most readers. Many articles describe the pleasurable sensations of contractions: the squeezing and releasing motion of muscles, both those we control and those we may not be aware of.

This may be an appropriate point to discuss another issue, multiple orgasms. There is widespread belief that women have a much greater capacity for multiple orgasms than men. Some authorities go so far as to say that women are sexually "insatiable." Others claim that the so-called multiple orgasms are actually a series of sensations properly described as erotic but not orgasmic. Whether or not all the multiple-orgasm reports are credible—and I tend to respect the fact that people generally know what they themselves actually feel—the issue is relevant to the concept of sexual symmetry because it suggests that one sex is "sexier" than the other.

To reinforce my argument, it is acknowledged that both men and women can and do have multiple orgasms. The men who do tend to be quite young. Age is not as significant a factor in women.* The issue

*We have been led to believe that men reach their sexual peak at eighteen or so and then very gradually begin to decline, whereas women are supposed to reach their peak at twenty-five to thirty and to retain their potential into quite old age—a phe-

does not seem to revolve around arousability, orgasm itself, or ejaculation, but rather around rearousability.

In men, erection is achieved rather quickly, and after orgasm and ejaculation it subsides just as quickly, the penis returning to its "resting" state almost immediately, or in younger men within several minutes. In women, the C.U.V. response may not be achieved quite as quickly, and it appears that it usually takes longer for the swollen tissues of the C.U.V. organ to become deflated and for the various parts to return to their normal bifurcated "resting" state. In this more prolonged phase, the female organ may still have the capacity for being rearoused to another or a series of orgasms. In those males who happen to experience a similar delayed deflation of the penis, rearousal to full erection (and orgasm) certainly is not unknown.

Reports of the multi-orgasmic experiences of men indicate that the supply of male sexual fluids gives out, so that in later orgasms there is usually no ejaculation—just the sensation of orgasm. It is possible that this may be true also in the case of women who report multi-orgasms.

It may be that when some women experience orgasm, they temporarily stop, or the stimulation is terminated before the ejaculatory response is elicited. Conversely, depending on types of stimulation, a woman who has awareness of her ejaculatory response and has repeated ejaculations without or-

---

nomenon Mark Twain called "God's horrid jest." It is nevertheless a well-known fact that many women find older men sexually attractive, which suggests that men can remain active lovers—and certainly become more skilled—later in life.

gasm may feel very gratified but not satiated. In fact, overstimulation of the systems linked to ejaculatory release, while not inhibiting orgasm, may make it more difficult for a woman to achieve one. While these mechanisms are not yet fully understood, they may be under hormonal control.

My original work on female ejaculation established that men and women, both having prostate gland structures, have the potential to ejaculate fluids during sexual stimulation—thereby removing the last barrier to acceptance of a symmetry of sexual function as well as form between a man and a woman. As I have already explained, because the woman's glans and urethral opening are inside the vagina during coitus, an ejaculation-like spurting of fluid from the urethral opening is blocked by the penis, making the phenomenon of ejaculation in women discernible only by increased wetness.

Deflation—the draining of blood and fluids from the genitals—usually seems to be dramatically more rapid in the male.

Satiety, which follows the four phases just described, defines a psychological state. The word itself is derived from a Latin word *(satietas)* which is related to the Anglo-Saxon *saed* meaning "sad." (Galen wrote that "every animal is sad after coitus, except the human female and the rooster.") In current usage, "satiety" means being completely satisfied and implies that all desire is gone for the time being.

Sexual satiety in the male but not necessarily in the female is popularly believed to have a physiological basis. In my opinion, it is only common sense to see that both men and women who experience a sequence of sexual sensations that bring about complete gratification experience that state.

There is a Chinese proverb about a fisherman who starts out with two canoes, one foot in each. Writing about the physiology of passion, I find myself thinking of the inevitable fate of the fisherman and the need to say something about the unity of mind and body, brain and genitals, that is inherent in orgasm.

The brain has different centers of control but functions as a unit. Like the brain, the sexual organs—distinct in themselves as body parts—during passion function as one, with each other and with the brain. The C.U.V. sensory organ functions in unison with muscles, blood vessels, and the nerves from which all information flows to the brain. The sensations we experience during sexual passion from the senses—what we see, taste, hear, smell, and, above all, touch—register in the brain centers through the nerves via the spinal cord and through a glandular/hormonal channel via the bloodstream. For the most part, we are not conscious of these controls. But we know that we have some conscious control over our sexual behavior and what we select to experience.

We know also something about the part of the brain (the outermost layer, called the cortex) involved in this selection. The genital/brain connection is not, however, a direct one-way passage but a two-way flow, back and forth, each influencing the other. That is why we pay a price sexually if we overstress the mental in our sexual experience or localize it too specifically in one spot or another of the genitals. It is somewhat like the irony of knowledge itself. When you know something so well that it has become a part of you, you can forget about it. It becomes part of the way you meet and respond to your experience.

A way to imagine what is going on during orgasm is to think of the brain as the seed and flower; the genitals as the root.

Colin Blakemore, a scientist who writes about the mechanics of the mind, tells us that perception cannot proceed without expectation.* If the brain is not familiar with something—doesn't "expect" something—we have to go through a process of familiarization. We build or "wire" into the brain certain expectations. We do this by repeating experiences that, in effect, "create" a neural pathway. But, even then, awareness can excite or inhibit impulses from brain cells. Each person's sexuality is linked to the awareness of his or her genitals. Some scientists have actually established a positive correlation between a woman's capacity for orgasm and her degree of awareness of her vagina and breasts; the woman who is highly orgasmic is likely to be one with a clear awareness of her sexual organs. Thus, scientific explanation that contributes to greater awareness in men and women does not diminish but rather enhances the spontaneity and pleasure of the sexual experience.

The question lovers ask each other—"Do you feel what I feel?"—is a classic one. The same question was addressed in a somewhat different, more competitive way in Greek mythology.

Zeus and Hera came close to battle over the eternal question, "Who feels the greater pleasure from

*Colin Blakemore, *Mechanics of the Mind* (Cambridge: Cambridge University Press, 1977).

coitus, man or woman?" Zeus argued that the female enjoyed sex more than the male; Hera, the opposite. To settle the dispute, they consulted Teiresias, who had been both man and woman.* His answer was:

If the sum of love's pleasure adds up to ten,
Nine parts go to women, only one to men.†

In contemporary thought on the subject, Teiresias and Zeus find support among those who say:

"Women are insatiable sexually."

"There are different kinds of female orgasm."

"Women have more contractions than men, and their orgasms last longer."

However, the sides are still being drawn. Others retort:

"Men get more pleasure from sex."

"Men have a greater sex drive, that has a more urgent need to be gratified."

"Men reach orgasm with less difficulty than women, and faster."

Psychologists, too, focus on the differences between the sexes rather than their similarities.

All the while, medical science has been presenting facts that assure us that the sexual responses of men and women match in every detail. Most of these

---

*Born a man, Teiresias had been turned into a woman as a punishment. After living as a woman for seven years, he was restored to his original sex.

†Pierre Grimal, *Dictionnaire de la Mythologie Grècque et Romaine* (Paris: Presses Universitaires de France, 1969), p. 459.

facts concern purely physical responses (of heart, blood, muscle)—things that scientists can measure. But lovers want to know more than that. They dream of sharing the same feelings and sensations. However, science has only just begun to provide information about what is going on sexually within the context of the brain/genital connection. In the past, people have been led to believe that women's orgasms are subjective—different from the vivid, objective orgasms men enjoy. Such statements confuse the matter and divert us from the truth.

The first fallacy is to equate orgasm with ejaculation, for scientists have established that they are two distinct phenomena. Christopher Bell points out that "orgasm [in men] has been reported to persist despite functional failure of ejaculation."[*] Alfred Kinsey reports that some castrated males claim that they continue to have orgasms, despite the fact that as a consequence of the removal of their testes the prostate and seminal vesicles degenerate and fluids therefrom are diminished.[†] John Money writes in some detail about the fact that orgasm can be independent of other factors in sexual function, citing reports of male patients with impairment of the reproductive system or unusual anomalies, who experience "dry-run" orgasm—a climax of intensified erotic sensation but without release of fluids. Conversely, Money explains that it is possible for a paraplegic to see himself ejaculating, though totally unaware of any somesthetic sensation of orgasm. "It

[*]Christopher Bell, "Autonomic Nervous Control of Reproduction," *Pharmacological Reviews* 24: 668, 1972.
[†]Kinsey, et al. *op. cit.,* pp. 744–745.

((*148*))

is a point of further interest," Money continues, "that the paraplegic, even though unable to manifest a reflex by induced ejaculation, may still be able to experience the subjective feelings of climax while asleep and having an erotic dream. This phantom orgasm in the dream happens without corresponding genitopelvic accompaniments."*

Another thing that contributes to confusion is the fact that even the definition of orgasm is still in question. Many people, like Dr. Kinsey, identify it as "the explosive discharge of neuromuscular tensions at the peak of sexual response." "Peak" is the key word here. Other authorities equate it more specifically with the release of blood from the genital tissues, or with the muscles that control contractions or spasms, while still others claim that orgasm may occur with or without muscular contractions.

Almost all of the definitions refer to orgasm as a single event, which may be one reason there are so many different views. As the new theory defines orgasm, there are three different stages of sensation. The different definitions may be based on reports of sensation perceived at one or the other of these different stages, which are usually experienced in so highly compressed a time frame—or one perceived as such—that it is difficult to separate them.

In orgasm, we experience at least three feelings:

- a sensation of a piercing compulsion—what Simone de Beauvoir attributes to the male only as "a piercing sensation of imminence," but which

*John Money, "Components of Eroticism in Man: II. The Orgasm and Genital Somesthesia," *The Journal of Nervous and Mental Disease* 132: 289–297, 1961.

the female may feel too—an awareness that orgasm is coming, an intense visceral "quickening" sensation that is both abdominal and genital; we know we are about to cross a threshold, there is no turning back, it is inevitable

- a sensation of erotic transport

- a sensation of ecstasy that rushes us across the threshold, where we re-find ourselves and return to our normal consciousness.

In these blissful moments, any difference between a man and a woman appears as a grain of sand beside the ocean.

CHAPTER 6

Flesh and Feelings: Insights and Oversights

To a woman in love, her private world seems the center of a very private universe. Yet what a woman thinks about her own body, her own individual nature, and the way men and women relate to one another are ideas that, as we have seen, have been shaped to a large extent by societal beliefs about these things.

Society's values influence scientific theories as well; by and large the two reinforce one another. Fallopio reinforced the idea of the female clitoris as a "kind of penis." As general knowledge about the deeper structures he had discovered became obscured, people came to think that the surface part was the whole clitoris, a small replica of the male's penis—a notion that helped to strengthen the already entrenched idea of women's genitals as inferior to men's.

((*151*))

Attitudes about women in general reflected a recurring theme of doubleness. From times that predate the Bible, woman was seen as representing both good and evil—the good being related to woman's reproductive role as nurse and nurturer, the bad with woman's sexual nature. Underlying both these ideas was the presumption of the superiority of the male.

In medical science, ideas about women can be traced, as we have also seen, to those of the early Greeks. Medicine grew out of philosophy, and the two were not particularly distinct in the minds of the ancient Greeks. John Burnet, the eminent scholar of antiquity, once described science in general as a process of "thinking about the world in a Greek way."* By this Burnet no doubt had in mind the Greek ideal that underlies the scientific approach—to use the powers of the mind in a rational way through a process of logical thought. But, unlike most modern scientists, the ancient Greeks set up dichotomies between good and evil, right and wrong, superior and inferior, mind and body. A dichotomy very much in evidence in the writings of the Greeks is that of male and female. In his book on the history of biology, Emanuel Radl describes Aristotle's philosophy as being strongly rooted in the recognition of the differences between the two sexes.†

Socrates in the *Republic* speaks for a society ruled by carefully selected and trained men and women. That is the Utopian ideal, but what comes through in the course of the Dialogues are the actual

*John Burnet, *Early Greek Philosophy,* 3rd ed. (London: Adam and Charles Black, 1920), p. v.

†Emanuel Radl, *The History of Biological Thought* (London: Oxford University Press, 1930), p. 106.

ideas that prevailed about the differences between the sexes: "A man and a woman who have a physician's mind have the same nature, but a man physician and a man carpenter have different natures" (Book V: 453). The differences in reproductive functions, of course, could not be overlooked, but if men and women differed only in that one respect—that "the female bears and the male begets"—more proof had to be produced to show that the woman was different from the man. The proof offered is in the form of a series of questions posed in such a way that the reader instantly knows what the outcome will be:

> Was this the basis of your distinction between the man naturally gifted for anything and the one not so gifted, that the one learned easily, the other with difficulty, that one with slight instruction could discover much of himself in the matter studied, but the other after much instruction and drill could not even remember what he had learned, and that the bodily faculties of the one adequately served his mind, while, for the other, the body was a hindrance? Were there any other points than these by which you distinguish the well endowed man in every subject and the poorly endowed? (455b) . . . Do you know, then, of anything practiced by mankind in which the masculine sex does not surpass the female on all these points?* (455c)

The conclusion is, of course, that "the one sex is far surpassed by the other in everything, one may say.

*Plato, I *Republic,* Book V, *The Collected Dialogues of Plato,* ed. by Edith Hamilton and Huntington Cairns, trans. by Paul Shorey (Princeton, N.J.: Bollingen Series, Princeton University Press, 1963), p. 694.

Many women, it is true, are better than many men in many things, but broadly speaking, it is as you say" (455d). If a man lived righteously, Plato goes on, he would be rewarded with an eternal existence—an eternal "blessed and congenial existence" in his native star in the universe. If, on the other hand, he lived an unrighteous and cowardly life on earth, at the time of his second birth he would face the punishment of being turned into a woman (455d).

In *Timaeus,* Plato explains the creation of the universe and the laws of generation, which include the same idea about the fate of men who were cowards or who led unrighteous lives (that is, those who let themselves be "conquered" by human emotions rather than conquering them by the faculty of reason). At the time of their second birth, as a punishment they would be changed into women.* Those who did not change their ways in this second life faced a somewhat worse fate; they would be changed into some animal (42c). Through Plato, the hierarchy of creatures set forth—men first, women next, and then the animals—influenced ideas about life and relationships between the sexes for many centuries to come. It is in this same work that Plato states, "Since human nature is two-fold, the superior sex is that which should be designated man" (42).†

In the view of the renowned science historian

---

*Plato, *Timaeus. The Collected Dialogues of Plato,* ed. by Edith Hamilton and Huntington Cairns, trans. by Paul Shorey. (Princeton, N.J.: Bollingen Series, Princeton University Press, 1963), p. 1171.

†George Sarton, *A History of Science* (Cambridge, Mass.: Harvard University Press, 1952), p. 423.

George Sarton, the influence of *Timaeus* upon later times was "enormous and essentially evil" because the work was accepted as scientific and "errors and speculations are never more dangerous than when they are offered to us under the cloak of science."* In Sarton's opinion, "Plato does not seem to have realized that married love involves a peculiarly intimate relation between two persons." He continues, "Whenever he idealized sexual desires—and he did so frequently—whenever he thought about struggle between spirit and the flesh, whenever he took a romantic view of love, his background was not heterosexual but homosexual." About Plato the man, Sarton writes, "Platonic love for him was the sublimation of pederasty; true love is called in *Symposium* (211n) the right method of boy loving." As Sarton explains, "Plato was not necessarily a pederast in the physical sense, but he was almost certainly homosexual. . . . He was somewhat of a woman hater. That is revealed to us many times in his writings." But we must assume, Sarton concludes, "that the average man in Greece, as in our own day, was inclined to love women and to beget children."†

Readers of Sigmund Freud who are also familiar with the writings of the early Greeks can see the link between some of his ideas and theirs. The contemporary psychologist H. J. Eysenck suggests that "perhaps the most famous of all is Plato's image of the tripartite division of the mind into the rider controlling an obedient and socialized horse and another, undisciplined and vicious one" and Freud's notion of

*George Sarton, *op. cit.*
†Ibid., p. 425.

ego, super-ego, and id.* The ego, like the rider of the chariot, tries to control or resolve the tensions between the id and the super-ego, which can be like two unruly horses pulling in different directions. The id is the unconscious, the part of the psyche that controls the libido, or sex drive, which Freud considered to be the source of all energy. The ego perceives what is going on and tries to do something about it. Problems arise when the unconscious impulses of the id interfere with the function of the ego. Freud believed that in order to resolve inner conflict an individual has to deal with these two forces.

The philosopher Martin Buber, a Viennese like Freud and only about twenty years his junior, wrote in the tradition of the Hasidic Jews.† In *I and Thou,* he describes a twofoldness that runs through the whole world, through each person and each human activity. Buber, like Freud in the original German, uses the terms "I/It." A third Viennese, the psychologist and writer Bruno Bettelheim, points out in his reinterpretation of Freudian theory, *Freud and Man's Soul,* that Freud "chose words that are among the first words used by every German child"—the words "I" (*ich,* in German) and "it" *(es)* which he used in the noun form as "the I" and "the it."‡ Bettel-

*H. J. Eysenck, *The Experimental Study of Freudian Theories* (London: Methuen, 1973), p. 391.

†Hasidism was a religious revivalist movement of popular mysticism among Jews in France and Germany in the Middle Ages that reached a peak in the second half of the twelfth century. Another Hasidic religious movement became widespread in the eighteenth and nineteenth centuries among Jewish families in Eastern Europe. The same mystical beliefs were revived once again in the 1920s by Buber.

‡Bruno Bettelheim, *Freud and Man's Soul* (New York: Vintage Books, Random House, 1984), p. 53.

heim rightly criticizes the Latin depersonalization of Freud's terms by Freud's first English translators, and quotes Freud himself, who stated that his purpose in using these two simple words was "to keep in contact with the popular mode of thinking." Of course, Freud also used Greek terms, but he somehow succeeded in making even those words—such as "psyche," "erotic," "neurotic"—become part of the world's vocabulary.

Freud himself is quoted in Lionel Trilling's *The Liberal Imagination* as having said that "he disclaimed the right to be called the discoverer of the unconscious, saying that whatever he may have done for the systematic understanding of the unconscious, the discovery properly belonged to the literary masters."* Freud explains "how closely the enlarged concept of sexuality of psychoanalysis coincides with the Eros of divine Plato."† In a later work, Freud writes, "In its origin, function, and relation to sexual love, the 'Eros' of the philosopher Plato coincides exactly with the life-force, the libido of psychoanalysis."‡ And Freud, like Plato, never questioned the assumption that that life force, or libido, was mascu-

*Lionel Trilling, *The Liberal Imagination: Essays on Literature and Society* (New York: Harcourt Brace Jovanovich, 1979), p. 153.

†Sigmund Freud, *Three Essays on the Theory of Sexuality* (1905), The International Psycho-Analytical Library, No. 57, ed. by John D. Sutherland; trans. and ed. by James Strachey (London: The Hogarth Press and the Institute of Psycho-Analysis, 1974), XVIII.

‡Sigmund Freud, *Group Psychology and the Analysis of the Ego* (1921), The Standard Edition of the Complete Works of Sigmund Freud, Vol. XVIII, trans. and ed. by James Strachey (London: The Hogarth Press and the Institute of Psycho-Analysis, 1955), p. 91.

line. Freud considers the libido, and everything associated with activity, as masculine, and everything associated with passivity as feminine. This idea of an active/passive dichotomy between the sexes reflected in Freud's theories comes straight from Aristotle, as does his more fundamental philosophy rooted in an emphasis on the differences between the sexes.

Another significant Greek influence on Freudian concepts is Greek mythology. One obvious example is Freud's concept of narcissism, a form of neurosis in which one has an exceedingly high regard for his own looks, body, and behavior. Freud's idea was that narcissism is an exaggeration of the self-love one normally feels. A student of the classics, Freud based this idea and the name on the Greek myth of Narcissus, who fell in love with his own reflection in a pool of water and spent his life gazing at it until he was changed into a flower. His fate was considered to be a punishment for spurning the love of Echo, a nymph who was silenced except for the power to repeat the words of others.

More central to Freud's ideas is the neurosis he called the Oedipus complex, a name adopted from the drama by Sophocles, *Oedipus the King.* According to Freud's theory, the complex involves a boy's love for his mother and jealousy/hatred for his father, feelings that lead to the boy's fear of castration. In normal individuals, this boyhood complex is resolved; but in neurotics, these impulses and an accompanying sense of guilt are never resolved. In the neurotic personality, they become repressed in the unconscious, are carried over into adulthood, and are projected onto other relationships.

Another form of neurosis identified by Freud was the conversion of unconscious conflict into symbolic bodily symptoms linked to sexual repression. Since women around the turn of the century were usually more sexually repressed than men, the condition was more often diagnosed in female patients than in males. According to Freud's theory, a woman who had trouble swallowing, but who had no evidence of any organic disease, could be experiencing the symptom because she was resisting unconscious fellatio impulses; pains in the hands were linked with repressed impulses to masturbate. In addition to pains in various parts of the body, the patient might report any number of other symptoms, such as weakness, spasms, coughing, or shortness of breath. Today this neurosis is called "conversion reaction," but in Freud's time it was known as "hysteria."

Hysteria and the idea of the wandering uterus mentioned earlier were first described in Plato's *Timaeus*. And one finds in Plato's description the exact same explanation of the cause of hysteria that Freud attributes to the disorder—sexual repression.

Plato describes the "private parts" of men and women and likens both penis and womb to disobedient creatures dominated by frenzied lusts. He characterizes the uterus as an "animal within" that is desirous of procreating children, which, "when remaining unfruitful long beyond its proper time, gets discontented and angry, and wandering in every direction through the body, closes up the passage of the breath and, by obstructing respiration, drives them to extremity, causing all varieties of disease,"* until at length, he concludes, the desire and love of the

*Plato, *Timaeus, op. cit.,* p. 1210.

man and woman bring them together (91c). Freud, of course, believed that to a major extent hysteria and all neurotic behavior were caused by frustration and anxiety in a person's sexual life. When Greek philosophers described sexual passion as "a form of madness," they did not mean to suggest by that phrase any real neurosis, but had in mind the artless actions and impulsive utterances so characteristic of an individual who falls passionately in love and whose irrational behavior makes the person appear in the eyes of others the consummate fool.

The classical roots of Freud's psychoanalytic theory are discussed by Dr. Ishak Ramzy, of the Menninger Foundation, who advises, "Whenever students of Freud find it hard to follow one part or the other of his theories, it would probably be of help to go back to some of Aristotle's doctrines.... For Freud, as for Aristotle, everything has to have matter and form." Ramzy pays tribute to Aristotle as "the inventor of formal logic which deals with reasoning as such, irrespective of its content," and he attributes Freud's ability to present lucid supporting arguments for his own ideas to this influence of Aristotle. Of Freud, Ramzy explains, "If any of his theories are unacceptable, this is not due to the way he argued it, but to the premises he started with."*

With this thought in mind, let us look at those ideas of Freud's and their possible sources that are relevant to the three issues we are examining: the origins of views on the female sexual anatomy, the

*Ishak Ramzy, "From Aristotle to Freud: A Few Notes on the Roots of Psychoanalysis," *Bulletin of the Menninger Clinic,* 1956, 20: 120, 121.

characterization of the female sex, and views on the relationship between the sexes.

"Anatomy is destiny," Freud tells us in his famous paraphrase of a remark of Napoleon's.* Freud was referring specifically to the female sex, but he was not thinking of the early medical view, *"Tota mulier in utero"* (The uterus *is* the woman)†—the belief that the birth process ruled a woman's life. Rather, Freud had in mind female sexual anatomy. His idea was that a woman's sense of herself was determined in her childhood by certain psychological responses that, in his view, were the inevitable psychological result of the difference between the female clitoris and the male penis. In "The Passing of the Oedipus-Complex," he writes: "The little girl's clitoris behaves at first just like a penis, but by comparing herself with the boy playfellow the child perceives that she has come off short and takes this fact as ill treatment and as a reason for feeling inferior."‡ In one sentence Freud has encapsulated his idea of a polarization of the sexes and a view of the female sex as inferior to the male—an inferiority that he believed little girls themselves automatically felt and accepted because of "organ inferiority," which he based on the premise of a penis/clitoris equation, now revealed as false.

Freud went on to reinforce the idea of the polarization of the sexes by an analysis of the difference

*Sigmund Freud, "The Passing of the Oedipus-Complex" (1924), in *Sexuality and the Psychology of Love,* ed. Philip Rieff (New York: The Macmillan Company, 1963), p. 180.

†A literal translation would read, "All of the woman is in the uterus."

‡Freud, *op. cit.,* p. 180.

between them based on the "doubleness" of sexuality in the female and its "singleness" in the male. The male "has only one principal sexual zone—only one sexual organ—whereas [the female] has two: the vagina, the true female organ, and the clitoris, which is analogous to the male organ."* Freud, however, regarded the clitoris as an inferior bodily organ and in one of his lectures described it as an "atrophied penis."† The active (male)/passive (female) dichotomy is another idea Freud used to describe the difference between the sexes. Since the sexual drive is always active, Freud associated it with masculinity. In Freud's opinion, "the libido is regularly and lawfully [his own word] of a masculine nature, whether in the man or in the woman."‡ Through this line of reasoning, Freud extended the association of maleness to the female clitoris. "Female genitality must come in childhood, centered principally in the clitoris," he wrote. "If one wishes to understand how the little girl becomes a woman, he must follow up the further destinies of this clitoris excitation. . . . If the woman finally submits to the sexual act, the clitoris [though an atrophied penis] becomes stimulated, and its role is to conduct the excitement to the adjacent genital parts; it acts here like a chip of pine wood, which is utilized to set fire to the harder wood. It

*Sigmund Freud, "Female Sexuality" (1931), in *Sexuality and the Psychology of Love,* ed. Philip Rieff, p. 197.

†Sigmund Freud, Standard Edition, Vol. XXII, "New Introductory Lectures of Psycho-Analysis" (1933 [1932]), "Dissection of the Psychical Personality," tr. and ed. by James Strachey, *op. cit.* (1964), p. 65.

‡Sigmund Freud, "The Transformations of Puberty" (1905), in *The Basic Writings of Sigmund Freud,* tr. and ed. by A. A. Brill. (New York: Random House, 1938), p. 612.

often takes some time before this transference is accomplished and during this transfer the young wife remains anesthetic."*

Freud offered the idea that a theoretical "male" clitoral response may be transferred to a "female" vaginal response as evidence of a sharp difference between the sexes, a difference predicated upon the acceptance of the age-old theme of doubleness in the female.

Freud perceived this doubleness not only in the female's anatomy but also in her sexual development.

> The sexual life of the woman is regularly split up into two phases, the first of which is of a masculine character, while only the second is specifically feminine. Thus in female development there is a process of transition from the one place to the other [from clitoris to vagina] to which there is nothing analogous in males. A further complication arises from the fact that the clitoris with its masculine character continues to function in later female sexual life in a very variable manner, which we certainly do not as yet fully understand.†

Freud's idea was that the antithesis between the clitoral function and the vaginal function set female development apart from that of the male. "In maleness is concentrated subject, activity, and the possession of a penis; femaleness carries on the object, and passivity. The vagina becomes valued henceforth as an asylum for the penis; it comes into the inheritance

*Freud, "The Tranformations . . . ," op. cit., pp. 613–614.
†Freud, "Female Sexuality," op. cit., p. 197.

of the mother's womb."* This active-passive dichotomy is again straight from Aristotle, as is the more
fundamental philosophy rooted in an emphasis on
the differences between the sexes.

One of the major influences in the development
of the male, according to Freud, is the boy's first sight
of the female genital region. When the boy sees this
for the first time, he does not perceive the doubleness
Freud attributed to it, rather, he "sees nothing."
Freud explains that "it is not until later, when some
threat of castration has obtained a hold on the boy
that the observation becomes important to him."†
The boy, like all boys, had always thought that everyone, male and female, had a penis just like his own.
So he thinks the girl must have lost her penis, and if
it could happen to her, it could also happen to him.
He becomes sexually intimidated by this threat of
castration, which leads to two reactions: "horror of
the mutilated creature or triumphant contempt for
her."‡ The term "mutilated" here is the same word
Galen used to describe the female anatomy, which
association perhaps Freud first discovered in Galen.
Freud's portrayal of children makes them seem like
little Adams and Eves, whose loss of innocence from
knowledge of each other's genitals leads to their psychological fall: the boy, thinking the girl is mutilated,
fears losing his penis; the girl, accepting her mutila-

*Sigmund Freud, "The Infantile Genital Organization of the
Libido" (1923), in *Sexuality and the Psychology of Love,* ed.
Philip Rieff, p. 175.
   †Sigmund Freud, "Some Psychological Consequences of the
Anatomical Distinction Between the Sexes" (1925), in *Sexuality
and the Psychology of Love,* ed. Philip Rieff, p. 187.
   ‡Ibid., p. 187.

tion, envies the boy's superior organ and wants to mutilate it.

Freud contends that "the conviction finally won that the woman has no penis often produces in the male a lasting depreciation of the other sex," and "it is of little help to the child when biological science agrees with his preconception [i.e., the boy's earlier idea that everyone has a penis] and recognizes the feminine clitoris as the real substitute for the penis."* Freud is proposing here, if I interpret him correctly, that even if the boy were to be informed of the "fact" of science—that the little girl's clitoris is the female equivalent of the penis—it would not change the "triumphant contempt" he feels for the female because of her "organ inferiority." According to Freud's psychoanalytic theory, the boy's development is shaped by the uninformed subjective ideas that come into his mind as a direct experience of his senses, rather than by ideas based on facts. In this case, the boy's specific castration idea demonstrates exactly Freud's idea of a dualistic genital organization of the libido according to which "the antithesis runs: a male genital organ or a castrated condition."† This is a direct descendant of the ancient idea of the primacy of the penis and follows the same dualistic mind-set.

Most of this first appeared in print in English in the 1920s. Since then there have been six decades of

*Sigmund Freud, "Infantile Sexuality" (1905), in *The Basic Writings of Sigmund Freud,* tr. and ed. by A. A. Brill, p. 595.

†Sigmund Freud, "The Infantile Genital Organization of the Libido" (1923), in *Sexuality and the Psychology of Love,* ed. Philip Rieff, p. 175.

writings on the subject of penis envy, and if one tries to make a fair evaluation of the consensus reached by others, it is that the issue appears to be a moot one. There is no point in questioning whether Freud reported accurately what he observed in his female patients, but, as he himself conceded, his opinion could be maintained only if his findings, which he admitted were based on no more than a handful of cases, turned out to have general validity. "If not," he wrote, "they would remain no more than a contribution to our knowledge of the different paths along which sexual life develops."*

Has Freud's penis-envy theory met the test of universality? Recently, Evelyne Sullerot has commented that penis envy did create "startling psychological sufferings in one or two generations of women of bourgeois environment."† It is generally agreed, however, that penis envy is not a universal part of normal female psychosexual development. A great deal of fuss has been made out of what could be perceived as a simple confusion between "envy of" and "desire for." A woman may dream about a man's genitals, just as a man may dream about a woman's, but as Eysenck succinctly sums it up, "as regards the dreams of women, how can we say that the appearance of phallic symbols indicates penis *envy* rather

---

*Evelyne Sullerot, "The Emotional State in Sexuality and Reproduction," in L. Carenza and L. Zichella, eds., *Emotion and Reproduction*. Fifth International Congress of Psychosomatic Obstetrics and Gynecology, Vol. 20A (London and New York: Academic Press, 1979), p. 94.

†Sigmund Freud, "Some Psychological Consequences of the Anatomical Distinction Between the Sexes" (1925), in *Sexuality and the Psychology of Love,* ed. Philip Rieff, p. 193.

than penis *interest?* It may be that women want a penis *in* them, not *on* them."*

Eysenck in the same paper reviews in detail the Hall and Van de Castle study, which is "particularly important to Freudian theory because it is apparently the *only* study that has been widely accepted as evidence for the penis-envy concept."† He concludes that the study cannot be taken as a validation for the castration complex.

A number of reinterpretations of the theory tried to shift its meaning from envy of the actual penis to envy of the male's position of dominance in the society, a so-called secondary penis envy, but Freud himself, referring to Karen Horney's 1926 paper on the subject,‡ dismissed such an interpretation: "This does not agree with the impression that I myself have formed."§ He reemphasized his belief that female "striving for masculinity" found its earliest expression in the little girl's desire for a penis, and that therefore that striving should be called "penis envy," as he had originally named it.

If Freud has taught us anything, he has taught us not to forget the importance of the individual and his or her own experiences, the nature and quality of which may be peculiar to that one individual. In this regard, Freud differs from the medical approach, which in establishing certain norms places its em-

*Eysenck, *The Experimental Study of Freudian Theories,* p. 166.

†Ibid., p. 167.

‡Karen Horney, "The Flight from Womanhood: The Masculinity Complex in Women as Viewed by Men and by Women," *International Journal of Psychoanalysis,* 7:324–329, 1926.

§Freud, "Female Sexuality," *op. cit.,* p. 211.

phasis on averages, or the mean. In medicine, physicians can learn from observing abnormal cases. By looking to pathology, the physician can detect quantitative characteristics of, say, the anatomy more plainly than in the normal, and can come up with a rational explanation of certain physical phenomena. Freud's theory emerged out of a similar approach but differs in his follow-through logic. Medical practitioners use the approach to gain insight, then use that insight to differentiate between the normal and the abnormal. Freud proposes that the insights gained from pathology—or in Freud's theories, many times, from neurosis—have implications for the course of normal psychosexual development.

What makes us do what we do? Freud held fast to his theory that all of us are motivated by our sexual impulses. And by identifying sexuality as part of normal child development, he was able to use examples from childhood to show that sexual function and reproductive function are not necessarily related.

In 1922, John Dewey wrote about the great evils of the artificial simplification of human nature into "a definite collection of primary instincts which may be numbered, catalogued and exhaustively described one by one. . . . Just now another simplification is current, all instincts go back to the sexual, so that *cherchez la femme* (under multitudinous symbolic disguises) is the last word of science with respect to the analysis of conduct."* Today psychology is not so one-sided.

Freud himself wrote, "The edifice of psycho-

*John Dewey, *Human Nature and Conduct: An Introduction to Social Psychology* (New York: Henry Holt and Co., 1922), pp. 132–133.

analytical doctrine which we have erected is in reality but a superstructure, which will have to be set on its organic foundation at some time or other; but this foundation is still unknown to us." Freud was referring to the lack of a chemical foundation for his sexual libido theory and specifically stated that "the chemistry of sexuality is a term without content; we know nothing about it."*

A great deal more is known today about the sex-linked hormones of androgen and estrogen, both of which are present in males and females, but that knowledge, too, is far from complete. We still know very little about the relationship between hormones and mood, for instance, let alone the complexities of what goes on hormonally during sexual stimulation. Interacting hormonal and psychological factors undoubtedly affect sexual behavior, but conclusive studies have not been conducted. Androgens are thought to be the libido-enhancing hormones, and estrogen therapy in the treatment of postmenopausal women enhances the production of sexual fluids.

Freud was prophetic in recognizing the critical role of chemicals in sexual function. He had started out with the idea of trying to construct a model of the mind based on neurophysiology. Once he came to realize how limited knowledge was as to the functioning of the central nervous system, he had to abandon the project. While his psychoanalytical theory has neither a hormonal nor a neurological base, it does have a psychological one, which he formulated

*Freud, "The Common Neurotic State," Introductory Lectures on Psycho-Analysis, Part III, *General Theory of the Neuroses* (1917 [1916–17]), Standard Ed., Vol. XVI, tr. and ed. by James Strachey, 1963, p. 388.

from his observation of patients and analyses of their thinking. The fact remains, however, that some of his own ideas about women and the relationship between the sexes were influenced by a false notion of the female sexual anatomy.

Psychology and psychiatry have played vital roles in lifting the veils from repressive notions of female sexuality, but, at the same time, it is possible that a philosophical lag can be discerned in some of their theories that relate to attitudes about the sexes. Both disciplines have been influenced by psychoanalytical ideas about the relationship between men and women.* Within each of these fields, the nature/nurture controversy is an issue that divides thinking. Some believe that we are already formed psychologically at birth and who we are biologically conditions how we shape ourselves—what we choose to do and experience. Others believe that we come into this world open to psychological conditioning by the culture into which we are born. Still others recognize the validity of both approaches and are concerned with what goes on inside the "self" and also between the self and the societal environment. Psychoanalytic theory was rooted in the idea that physi-

*Psychology, which evolved out of philosophy, is defined as the science of the psyche, or mind, or of mental processes. Psychiatry is a branch of medicine, dedicated to the study and treatment of mental, emotional, and personality disorders, especially those that are the result of difficult relationships with "significant others." Psychoanalysis, originated by Freud, is a specialization in the field of psychology; its approach is to analyze the workings of the mind through techniques such as free association of words and thoughts and interpretation of dreams.

ological functions such as hunger, thirst, and, most of all, sexual drive are what affect motivation; that to understand motivation, it is necessary to have techniques to "tap" the unconscious. So much emphasis was placed on the unconscious and sex in psychoanalytical theory that the importance of conscious mental processes came to be minimized. As a reaction to this one-sidedness, there has been a return to the original concern of psychology, which was the understanding of the mind through study of the self and mental processes.

William James, often called the father of modern psychology, defined the self as the "sum total of all that [an individual] can call his, not only his body and his psychic powers, but his clothes, and his house, his wife and children, his ancestors and friends, his reputation and works, his lands and horses and yacht and bank account."* All these things are experienced as part of oneself (by male and female, we might add) and anything that affects any one of them affects one's self-esteem.

Negative qualities attributed to individuals can very well affect how they perceive and evaluate themselves, which in turn affect their self-esteem— that is, their sense of pride and worth. Contemporary psychiatrists recognize that any blow to self-esteem affects one's self-image. If that blow is linked in some way to a person with whom one is involved emotionally, it can deeply alter one's ideas about oneself— whether one is desirable or undesirable, normal or

*William James, *The Principles of Psychology*, Vol. I (London: Macmillan and Co., Ltd., 1890), p. 291.

abnormal. Such ideas may lead to a state of general anxiety about one's sexuality, and a vicious circle is set in motion. Psychiatrist Silvano Arieti recognizes that "sexual gratification, deprivation, and dysfunction are phenomena that affect the whole self-image, and the self-image often affects sexual function."*

Human nature is such that when we are happy in our sexual lives, we rarely dwell on the fact—we just enjoy it. But when something goes wrong, we not only feel deprived, we tend to think more about it and to feel generally diminished. "Sexual deprivation may be unpleasant, but the image that the sexually deprived person may form of himself as a sexual object can be much more traumatic," Arieti explains. "Is he sexually adequate? Is he sexually desirable?"† Male impotence, for example, can affect both partners. When a man can't achieve erection, he may begin to think of himself as inadequate sexually. A physical lapse of this sort may be just that, something of a very temporary nature; but the negative self-image the man imposes upon himself can develop a devastating, more lasting psychological effect.

The man usually recovers from the initial blow to esteem that brought on the impotence in the first place, but the trauma of inability to perform sexually makes him insecure and fearful of repetition. This insecurity and sense of sexual inadequacy may have a more lasting effect on his virility. Depending on

*A. L. Arieti, *Selected Papers of Silvano Arieti* (New York: Brunner/Mazel Publishers, 1978), p. 354.

†Silvano Arieti, *The Intrapsychic Self: Feeling and Cognition in Health and Mental Illness* (New York: Basic Books, 1976), p. 163.

personal values and personality factors, there is a whole range of possible ways in which the woman involved may react. A woman, misinterpreting the underlying causes of impotence in the male, may begin to question her own sexual attractiveness as a woman and to wonder if she is the one responsible.

A large majority of psychologists are practicing professionals—in clinical psychology, education, or the business world. Only a small percentage are primarily concerned with theory. Among contemporary theoretical writing, there is much less concern about sexual theory than there was twenty or forty years ago. The profession nowadays is more concerned with the mental processes involved in language and learning, stages of individual development, including how we perceive and remember things, and the development of children. Psychologists who write about child development continue to present their ideas in the context of how similar or dissimilar to Freud's theories they are. Some come across as a blend of new theory mixed with attitudes that are strongly reminiscent of Freudian and Aristotelian ideas about primacy of the male anatomy and polarization of the sexes. For example, when considering children's awareness of genital differences, cognitive psychologists do not assume, as Freud did, either an infantile "phallic" sexuality or a central Oedipal complex with attendant castration fears. Cognitive development theory centers on the child's uncertainty about "anatomical constancy." As an expression of this uncertainty the child feels both fascinated and threatened, attitudes that, as has been described in writings on the subject, can also be perceived in men, women, and chimpanzees toward the maimed and deformed. According to cognitive theory, children tend to value things with which they can identify, and to perceive themselves as being identified with that which they value. As explained by the Swiss psychoanalyst Raymond de Saussure, "It also seems likely on purely cognitive grounds that both sexes would take the male anatomy as more basic in defining some sexually undifferentiated human-body schema, i.e., that the female body would be conceived as the negative of the masculine, rather than as a positive entity."*

Some of the above material was published in 1966, the year in which Natalie Shainess presented a paper entitled "A Reassessment of Feminine Sexuality and Erotic Experience" to the tenth annual meeting of the American Academy of Psychoanalysis.† Shainess was one of the first practitioners to point a finger at male bias among therapists and their tendency to equate self-assertiveness in women with aggression. She also recognized that it was all the more important to distinguish between the two characteristics in women, in light of the fact that women have

---

*See material in E. E. Maccoby, ed., *The Development of Sex Differences* (Stanford, Calif.: Stanford University Press, 1966).

Saussure's article, "Psychologie genetique et psychanalyse," appeared in the *Revue Française de Psychanalyse,* 6: 365–403, 1933. Saussure was a colleague of members of the Paris Psychoanalytic Society, founded in 1926 by a group of practitioners that included Marie Bonaparte. He was the first in the field to address the relation between psychoanalysis and the child development theories of Jean Piaget.

†Natalie Shainess, "A Reassessment of Feminine Sexuality and Erotic Experience," in Jules H. Masserman, ed., *Sexuality of Women, Science and Psychoanalysis.* (New York: Grune and Stratton, 1966).

been traditionally viewed as either passive, narcissistic, and masochistic, or aggressive, jealous, and penis-envying. At the discussion following the presentation of Dr. Shainess's paper, Dr. Joseph C. Solomon, a physician, addressed the issue of the dominance of male-oriented thinking in the profession: "Inasmuch as the psychoanalytic movement was begun by males, especially at a time when females were undervalued, it is easy to understand how it came about that the description of feminine sexuality was an absence of masculinity rather than possessing any attributes of a positive nature."*

The assumption seems to be that such ideas had been put behind once and for all, but, as described above, the evidence indicates that the ideas of the 1930s had survived into the 1960s. In the past two decades, a new era of thinking about women and the sexes has been introduced in Western society, and certainly individual psychologists, male and female, have responded to this change. Their response has been influenced by the prodding of feminist writers concerned about male bias within the profession, but it is principally through their practices that psychologists have become sensitively attuned to sex discrimination and bias against women, for they deal with the psychological aftermath of the damage done not only in the workplace and in the school but in family and love relationships.

Not every female voice within the profession is speaking out in rejection of a masculine-feminine duality. The thinking of some women psychologists remains within that traditional framework, their

*Shainess, *op. cit.*, p. 71.

major concern being to give greater value to those qualities of women they perceive as being intrinsically feminine. Some feminists, ironically, make the same kind of bipolar classifications of the sexes as the Greeks did. Sociobiologist Sarah Blaffer Hrdy is herself a feminist, but questions the feminist ideal of a sex "less egotistical, less competitive by nature, less interested in dominance, a sex that will lead us back to the 'golden age of queendoms, when peace and justice prevailed on earth.'" She thinks that is "a dream that may not be well founded." In Dr. Hrdy's view:

> Widespread stereotypes devaluing the capacities and importance of women have not improved either their lot or that of human societies. But there is also little to be gained from countermyths that emphasize woman's natural innocence from lust for power, her cooperativeness and solidarity with other women. Such a female never evolved among the other primates.*

On the other hand, the women psychologists of whom I speak contend that there is a distinctively female way of thinking about one's life and relationships and that women tend to focus on such things, whereas men concern themselves with broader societal issues. Their theories about the sexes may differ from those of the ancients, but the difference is largely that they speak for greater recognition of women's voices; they are hardly speaking for a fundamental change in the classical polarization of the

*Sarah Blaffer Hrdy, *The Woman That Never Evolved* (Cambridge, Mass., and London, Eng.: Harvard University Press, 1987), p. 190.

sexes. One is left to wonder if the profession has indeed succeeded in lifting itself out of the old ways of thinking about the sexes.

In a discussion about the scientific rationalistic way of looking at things, Albert Einstein advises, "It is just as well to state a thesis starkly and nakedly, if one wants to clear up one's mind as to its nature."* The psychology profession knows the importance of a positive self-image to an individual's well-being, but its old beliefs—"the female is the negative of the masculine, not herself an entity," the male is the primary model of reference, the dominant sex—die hard. Starkly and nakedly stated, the professional attitude toward the relationship between the sexes is part of a continuum of thought on the subject that can be traced back to Aristotle and the early Greek philosophers. Seemingly new directions present themselves, but on closer scrutiny they are like new accretions on an old shell, the core of which is the same attitude about the sexes that has existed for two thousand years.

*Albert Einstein, *Out of My Later Years* (New York: Philosophical Library, 1950), p. 21.

CHAPTER 7

Conclusion

Because each individual in the world is different from every other, it is difficult to generalize about sex. While some people may still be influenced by traditional ideas on the subject, others, especially younger people, may pay no attention to them. Certainly views about the relationship between the sexes have been changing radically since the end of World War II. More and more women are breaking away from what Virginia Woolf called the "looking-glass" image—women whose lives were only a reflection of their husbands'. More and more men as well as women believe that sexual relations should be based on a sense of mutuality, rather than dominance by one or the other sex.

But despite advances in knowledge about human sexuality in the past few decades, women still have to contend psychologically with the heritage of an earlier science of evasion, which denied female sexuality, and with a lingering confusion about the female sexual parts.

A great deal of confusion was caused by the old dualistic concept of "clitoris versus vagina." The

C.U.V. response puts such a basic misconception to rest. With awareness of the integrated, equally important functions of the three parts—clitoris, vagina, and urethra—couples will realize the limitations imposed on women's sexual potential if only one "spot" or another is thought to dominate female response. No longer will lovemaking tend to fixate on the clitoris, no longer will the urethra be thought of merely as a conduit for the release of urine, and no longer will the vagina be considered a void lacking in sensitivity. We realize now that all parts of the vagina are potentially alive with sensation—the entrance; the top, behind the cervix; the front, or roof; and the *rear* of the vagina as well.

The woman's glans has always been there, but awareness of its existence and capacity for excitation, along with that of the clitoris, should facilitate female orgasm and ejaculation. Furthermore, the naming of a structure is important for a number of obvious reasons. Names help to identify what one is talking about, aid in communication, and in themselves sharpen the awareness of one part as distinct from another. In the past, without a name for the woman's glans, a woman might have felt sensations in that area, but lacking any vocabulary to help identify them, she could not easily communicate exactly what she was feeling or why. Awareness of those sensations could, therefore, easily become diffused instead of sharpened. With the naming of the glans, the whole process is reversed. The woman knows why she is feeling such pleasurable sensations at the outermost part of the vagina. The man is more knowledgeable about what he is touching and stimulating in the woman and about the responses it will elicit.

And when the names of the comparable male and female parts are the same, lovers recognize one more physical way in which they can identify with each other and communicate the feelings that they share.

The new findings about female ejaculation provide a tangible basis for a more objective evaluation of female physiological responses to sexual stimulation. Among those who have commented upon the significance of this information are physiologist Julian M. Davidson of Stanford University and medical psychologist John Money of The Johns Hopkins Hospital. Commenting on my 1978 article cited earlier, Dr. Davidson wrote: "The observation that the female prostate may not be entirely vestigial, and the possibility that, in some women at least, it may be secretory, potentially removes the last barrier to consideration of the hypothesis that no qualitative differences exist between the male and female sexual response."* Dr. Money, who was one of the first medical scientists to encourage me in my initial research effort, pointed out that before this information was published, "it was believed that women were hyperphilic and abnormal if they claimed to ejaculate fluid at orgasm."†

With barriers removed and acceptance of the fact that female ejaculation is normal, women, as many have already reported, find their psychological well-being enhanced by a sense of confidence rather than doubt about a physiological phenome-

*J. M. Davidson and R. J. Davidson, *The Psychobiology of Consciousness* (New York: Plenum Press, 1980), p. 310.

†John Money, "The Development of Sexuality and Eroticism in Humankind," *The Quarterly Review of Biology,* 56 (4): December 1981, p. 395.

non which until very recently was usually diagnosed as incontinence, or automatically associated with injury or infection. Now that men recognize that women experience a little lag between orgasm and ejaculation, they should realize the special pleasure for both partners in sustaining stimulation in the woman who so desires it during those moments of post-orgasmic heightened sensation of the C.U.V. organ. Awareness of female ejaculation, of what excites it, of the importance of "bearing down" to help effect it, and of its sources, amounts, and timing in relation to orgasm (the two phenomena, orgasm and ejaculation, are rarely simultaneous in women) should help both women and their lovers to come to a better understanding of female sexuality.

We have been told how much alike men and women are sexually; now we know in much more explicit detail why. All this new information contributes to a conception that I believe is closer to the way in which most contemporary couples think about themselves—not as divided into the active and passive players, but as sexual partners creating and sharing in a relationship of interdependence.

Some of my colleagues have expressed curiosity about a few things, such as Lilith's preference for the superior coital position, the "gatekeeper" of the vagina, and simultaneous orgasm; in response, I offer a few details about how the information presented relates to these subjects.

Since Lilith's prediliction is one that is shared by quite a few real-life contemporary women, I should mention that more than psychological factors are involved; there may, in fact, be an anatomical basis for such preference. Women may not care at all about a hypothetical sense of dominance, or even about the psychological appeal of occasionally exchanging positions with their partners. Couples have pragmatically observed that with the woman on top, the vaginal-penile "fit" tends to accentuate stimulation of the roof of the vagina. Though supine, the man experiences maximum exposure of the penis to the vaginal caress; also, his hands are freer. The woman in this position is able effectively to control the proximity of the vulva to the pelvic area of the man in ways that can stimulate the exposed Lowndes crown. Alternatively, if she raises her body up and down or, bending forward with breasts touching, slides back and forth, she can by these movements control the squeezing action of the lower vagina to vary the place of impact and friction between penis and vagina.

Dr. Van de Velde, cited earlier, called this the "astride" position or "attitude of equitation." He mentioned that there may be anatomical peculiarities of individual structure which deny to certain women, or certain couples, this particular form of connection: "In the case of a comparatively short, inelastic or easily vulnerable vagina, the astride attitude involves too many drawbacks and even dangers." One reason for his caution may be that the position is known to encourage the deepest penetration of the penis—in other circumstances, a very desirable sensation. On the positive side, Dr. Van de Velde recognized that

> there are new possibilities of sensation here, which we have not met before. These arise because this attitude . . . permits full penetration of the male organ into the vagina. . . . The woman in

this attitude is able to move her pelvis and abdomen sideways [and] in all directions. [She can
move] in a straight line (sideways, or backwards
and forwards) . . . or with a circular "corkscrew"
motion of the pelvis. Both these methods give as
it were a different color-tint and timbre of erotic
pleasure; in the circular movement the pleasurable sensations, at least on the man's side, are the
stronger.*

This is, of course, but one position of the many that
provide the couple with an opportunity to discover
the movements that create great satisfaction for each
other.

Experienced men know how frustrating it can be
for both partners if the man attempts to insert the
penis before the woman is adequately aroused. On
the other hand, if he waits too long, the muscles that
surround the vagina may involuntarily begin to contract and make entry difficult, a condition of vaginal
tightness clinically known as vaginismus. In persistent cases, it is wise for a woman to consult a physician to be certain there is no underlying physical
disorder or organic cause. As uncomfortable and
disappointing as the experience of vaginismus can
be, a woman's capacity for orgasm by means other
than coital stimulation is not necessarily diminished, unless a corollary inhibition takes hold as a
result of fear of the pain or anxiety caused by psychological factors. In the absence of any medical problems, the present clinical approach is based on
educating the woman to control voluntary contraction and relaxation of the vaginal muscles, so that

*T. H. Van de Velde, *Ideal Marriage: Its Physiology and Tech-
nique,* pp. 222, 223.

she will first become at least comfortable with the sensations and ultimately will rediscover pleasure. Part of the program's success depends on knowledge of the physiology of sexual response, but much emphasis is given to analysis of intrapsychic conflict about sex that sets up a conditioned reflex. Many times negative attitudes about sex are attributed to these woman—they don't really like sex, or they are inhibited about "letting go" sexually. The partner of such a woman may begin to fear that she is resistant to him personally and is intentionally blocking him out, when ironically the fact may be that the woman is so intensely excited sexually that her responses to the man are extra fast. The vagina's capacity for clasping the penis is normally valued by male and female, but when the muscles that cause this highly erotic response go into action before the penis is introduced, troubles follow. If the woman's condition is caused by an accelerated C.U.V. response, such a situation would indicate that the couple might consider the need either for less stimulation of the woman's genitals than is customary in their pre-coital lovemaking, or for more stimulation of the male genitals in order to match the man's erection to the quickness of the woman's.

A woman's genitals need no longer be the "dark continent" of old. With awareness of the relatedness of male and female anatomy, a couple should be able to exert more control over the timing of stimulation. With greater knowledge of what is going on inside her body during the action of the muscles in the lower vagina and that of the pubococcygeus, which controls the surge a little higher up, a woman can derive more pleasure from the sensations that accompany the vaginal transformations and repositionings that bring about the C.U.V. response and erection.

"From an Unfortunate Necessity to a Cult of Mutual Orgasm," the title of an article cited by Carl Degler, sums up the changing views about sex in the century from 1830 to 1940.* In the second half of the twentieth century, Kinsey, writing in 1953, took things a step further—from mutual orgasm to simultaneous orgasm:

> Simultaneous orgasm for the two partners in a coital relationship derives its significance chiefly from the fact that the intense responses which the one partner makes at the moment of orgasm may stimulate the other partner to similarly intense response. Consequently simultaneous orgasm represents, for many persons, the maximum achievement which is possible in a sexual relationship.†

An ideal it may be, others say, but difficult to achieve. They believe simultaneous orgasm is not too likely an event in the actual experience of couples. Still others believe that sex should be free of any kind of goal orientation, lest compulsion set in and idealism turn to idolism. Whether simultaneous orgasm is considered an ideal, a rare event, or something best left to chance, most people would concede that if it happens, it does indeed give lovers a sense of exaltation in the realization that they can bring each other, as Kinsey suggests, to at least an approximately

---

*Michael Gordon's article, "From an Unfortunate Necessity to a Cult of Mutual Orgasm: Sex in American Marital Education Literature, 1830–1940," appears in James M. Henslin, ed., *Studies in the Sociology of Sex* (New York: Appleton-Century Crofts, 1971).

†Kinsey, et al., *op. cit.,* p. 372.

simultaneous peak of passion. Now through greater awareness of the vital parts involved in arousal and readiness for orgasm, such as the Lowndes crowns, the male clitoris, and the C.U.V. organ, men and women who desire the experience of coming in the same moments have an informed basis for exploring more sensitive timings to achieve it.

Lovers are concerned about the well-being of one another, and yet, being so emotionally vulnerable in the love state, frustrations fostered by lack of information can easily become disproportionately powerful in undermining those good feelings without which nothing very much can happen sexually. There is nothing simple about what goes on in the intimacies of sex. Men and women need as much insight as possible in living together through the ups and downs of sexual passion.

After the introduction of Freud's theories, sex was thought to be primarily motivated by drives and tensions of a quantitative nature. By the time of the sexual revolution in the 1960s, people were tending increasingly to equate sexual love with genital love. With attraction, desire, and arousal comes, without question, passion for genital closeness; but today sex is conceived as a more complex expression, involving biological factors and also the interplay between brain and genitals, emotions and eroticism—form, feelings, and function—which qualitatively affect one's sexual capacity, performance, orgasmic intensity, and facility, but which, at the same time, transcend genitality and determine the quality of one's life and relationships for better or for worse.

Studies that bridge science and sex should ideally be, I believe, mindful of the pluralistic nature of individuals and relationships and of the fact that what goes on between a woman and a man in the privacy and selective creativity of their lovemaking tends to elude the precision of laboratory models and measurement. Human beings are not "loving" automatons. The pervasive individuality of lives, the idiosyncratic nature of psychological and environmental factors that affect expression of each person's sexuality have to be more respected than they have been in the past. In keeping with this belief, how the new information I have presented is used by individuals is, in my opinion, best left to their own creative resources and individual preferences.

I hope this book will help couples to look at things in new ways. There is always a new way of perceiving ourselves and others. When a woman and a man look at each other now, it can be with a fresh awareness of how much alike their bodies are. And the discoveries that await them in identifying with each other on the physical level should help to give them a greater sense of mutuality in living their lives together.

APPENDIX A

Names and Definitions

The muscles linked with the sexual organs are named according to the part of the body where they originate: the *pubo*coccygeus—the pubic bone; the *ilio*coccygeus—the hipoccygeus—the hip bones; the *coccy*geus—the base of the spine.

PUBOCOCCYGEUS: arises from the pubic bone about 1.5 cm to each side from the center, forms an oval ring that surrounds the urethra, vagina, and rectum, attaching itself to the coccyx. The pubococcygeus is part of the so-called levator muscles, which also include the pubo-urethralis and the pubo-rectalis.

ILIOCOCCYGEUS: arises from the "white line" between the back of the pubic arch and the spine and inserts into the sides of the coccyx and the lower back.

COCCYGEUS: *(also called ischiococcygeus)*   arises from the bones we sit on and almost as a continuation of the levator muscles in the rear fills the space between the levators and inserts itself into a ligament along the side of the coccyx and the lower back.

Musculature of
the Sexual Organs

	FEMALE	PRESENT IN THE MALE
PERINEAL BODY: *(The only difference at this level is that the female PB contains the Bartholin glands, the male counterpart of which—the Cowper's glands— is set farther up in the next level.)*	• anal constrictors	Yes
	• superficial transverse	Yes
	• bulbospongiosum (covers bulbs)	Yes
	• ischiocavernosus (covers crura)	Yes
UROGENITAL DIAPHRAGM: *(This level is considered to be part of the perineum.)*	• deep transverse	Yes
	• constrictor of the urethra	Yes
		(Cowper's glands)

	FEMALE	PRESENT IN THE MALE
PELVIC DIAPHRAGM:	• pubococcygeus (pc)	Yes
(This level is in the middle and upper vagina.)	• iliococcygeus (ic)	Yes
	• coccygeus (ischiococcygeus)	Yes

Note: The pc and the ic (with urethral and rectal muscles as well) are as a group called the *levator ani,* which means "to raise the anus."

APPENDIX C

Galen's Homologues of Male and Female Sexual Organs

MALE	FEMALE
Scrotum	Fleshy part of vagina *(labia majora)*
Penis	Passageway of vagina
Penile prepuce *(foreskin)*	External genital parts *(labia minora)*
Prostate	Prostate

Arey's Male and Female Homologues

TABULATION OF UROGENITAL HOMOLOGIES

MALE	INDIFFERENT STAGE	FEMALE
Testis	Gonad	Ovary
(1)		(1) Cortex
(2) Seminiferous tubules		(2) Medulla (primary)
(3) Rete testis		(3) *Rete ovarii*
(1) *Mesorchium*	Genital ligaments	(1) Mesovarium
(2)		(2) Suspensory ligament of ovary
(3) *Ligamentum testis*		(3) Proper ligament of ovary
(4) *Gubernaculum testis* (caudal part)		(4) Round ligament of uterus
(5) *Gubernaculum testis* (as a whole)		(5) . . . .
(6)		(6) Broad ligament of uterus

APPENDIX D

MALE	INDIFFERENT STAGE	FEMALE
	Mesonephric collecting tubules	
(1) Efferent ductules; cranial *aberrant ductule*	(1) Cranial group	(1) *Epoöphoron; aberrant ductules*
(2) *Paradidymis;* caudal *aberrant ductule*	(2) Caudal group	(2) *Paroöphoron*
(1) *Appendix epididymidis*	Mesonephric (Wolffian) duct	(1) *Vesicular appendage*
(2) Ductus epididymidis		(2) *Duct of the epoöphoron*
(3) Ductus deferens; seminal vesicle		(3, 4) *Gartner's duct*
(4) Ejaculatory duct		
(5) Ureter, pelvis, etc.		(5) Ureter, pelvis, etc.
(1) *Appendix testis*	Müllerian duct	(1) Uterine tube
(2)		(2) Uterus
(3)		(3) Vagina (upper part?)
Seminal colliculus	Müller's tubercle	Hymen (site of)
(1) Bladder	Vesico-urethral primordium	(1) Bladder
(2) Upper prostatic urethra		(2) Urethra

Arey, Leslie B. *Developmental Anatomy: A Textbook and Laboratory Manual of Embryology.* Philadelphia: W. B. Saunders Co., 1965 (first published, 1924). Reprinted by permission.

APPENDIX D

MALE	INDIFFERENT STAGE	FEMALE
	Urogenital sinus	
(1) Lower prostatic urethra	(1, 2) Pelvic portion	(1) Vestibule (nearest vagina)
(a) *Prostatic utricle (vagina masculina)*		(a) Vagina (lower part, at least)
(b) Prostate gland		(b) *Para-urethral ducts;* urethral glands
(2) Membranous urethra		(2) Vestibule (middle part)
(3) Cavernous urethra	(3) Phallic portion	(3) Vestibule (between labia minora)
(a) Bulbo-urethral glands		(a) Vestibular glands (of Bartholin)
(b) Urethral glands (of Littré)		(b) Lesser vestibular glands
(1) Penis	(1) Phallus	(1) Clitoris
(a) Glans penis	(a) Glans	(a) Glans clitoridis
(b) Urethral surface of penis	(b) Lips of *urogen,* groove	(b) Labia minora
(c) Corpora cavernosa penis	(c, d) Shaft	(c) Corpora cavernosa clitoridis
(d) Corpus cavernosum urethrae		(d) Vestibular bulbs
(2) Scrotum	(2, 3) Genital swellings	(2) Labia majora
(3) Scrotal raphe		(3) Posterior commissure
(4)	(4) Median cranial swelling	(4) Mons pubis

The Lowndes Crowns Theory of Homologues of Male and Female Sexual Organs

FEMALE	MALE
Clitoris	Clitoris
Crown	*Crown*
Corpus	*Corpus*
Crura	*Crura*
Woman's glans	Penile glans
Carina of glans	Sulcus of glans *(corona)*
Prostatic glands	Prostate glands
Vagina	Penis

BIBLIOGRAPHY

Ashe, Geoffrey, *The Virgin*. London: Routledge & Kegan Paul, 1976.

Barthes, Roland, *A Lover's Discourse*. New York: Hill and Wang, 1978.

Berkow, S. G., "The corpus spongiosum of the urethra: its possible role in urinary control and stress incontinence in women," *American Journal of Obstetrics and Gynecology 65:* 346–351, 1953.

Bonney, Victor, "The female genital tract," in Charles Colby Choyce and J. M. Beattie, eds., *Systems of Surgery,* 2nd ed., Vol. II. New York: Paul B. Hoeber, 1923.

Bridges, E. Lucas, *The Uttermost Part of the Earth*. New York: E. P. Dutton, 1948.

Buber, Martin, *I and Thou*. New York: Charles Scribner's Sons, 1958 (Second edition).

Campbell, Joseph, *The Masks of God: Primitive Mythology*. New York: The Viking Press, 1974.

The Collected Dialogues of Plato, ed. by Edith Hamilton and Huntington Cairns, trans. by Paul Shorey. Princeton, N.J.: Bollingen Series, Princeton University Press, 1963.

de Beauvoir, Simone, *The Second Sex*. New York: Alfred A. Knopf, 1952.

de Graaf, Regnier, *New Treatise Concerning the Generative Organs of Women,* 1672. Annotated translation by H. B. Jocelyn and B. P. Setchell in *Journal of Reproduction and Fertility,* Supplement 17. Oxford: Blackwell Scientific Publications, 1972.

Dickinson, Robert Latou, *Human Sex Anatomy*. Baltimore: Williams & Wilkins Company, 1949.

Dorland's Illustrated Medical Dictionary. Philadelphia: W. B. Saunders, 1981.

Einstein, Albert, *Out of My Later Years*. New York: Philosophical Library, 1950.

BIBLIOGRAPHY

Elias, Hans, et al., *Histology and Human Microanatomy,* 4th ed. New York & Toronto: John Wiley & Sons, 1978.

Freud, Sigmund, "The Transformations of Puberty" (1905), Book III, *Three Contributions of the Theory of Sex,* in *The Basic Writings of Sigmund Freud,* trans. and ed. by A. A. Brill. New York: The Modern Library, Random House, 1938.

———, *Three Essays on the Theory of Sexuality* (1905). Standard edition, Vol. VII, 1953.

———, *Group Psychology and the Analysis of the Ego* (1921). Standard edition, Vol. XVIII, 1955.

Galeano, Eduard, *Memory of Fire: Genesis.* Trans. by Cedric Belfrage. New York: Pantheon Books, 1985.

Huisman, A. B., "Morphology of the female urethra," in Ulf Ulmsten, ed., *Female Stress Incontinence: Contributions to Gynecology and Obstetrics,* Vol. 10. Basel: S. Karger AG, 1983, pp. 1–31.

Jaszczak, S., and E.S.E. Hafez, "The Vagina and Infertility," in E.S.E. Hafez and T. N. Evans, eds., *The Human Vagina,* Vol. 2. Amsterdam and New York: North Holland Publishing Company, 1978.

Keibel, Franz, and F. P. Vall, *Human Embryology.* Philadelphia: J. B. Lippincott Company, 1912.

Kinsey, A. C., et al., *Sexual Behavior in the Human Female* Philadelphia: W. B. Saunders Co., 1953.

Malinowski, Bronislaw, *Sexual Life of Savages.* London: Routledge & Sons, 1929.

Masters, William H., and Virginia E. Johnson, *Human Sexual Response.* Boston: Little, Brown, 1966.

Muellner, S. Richard, "The Anatomies of the Female Urethra: A Critical Review." *Obstetrics & Gynecology,* 14 (4): October 1959.

Patai, Raphael, *The Hebrew Goddess.* New York: Avon Books, 1978.

Piersol, G. A., *Human Anatomy,* 9th ed. Philadelphia: J. B. Lippincott Company, 1930.

BIBLIOGRAPHY

Plath, Oreste, *Geografía del milo y la leyenda chilenos.* Santiago de Chile: Nascimento, 1973.

Radl, Emanuel, *The History of Biological Thought.* London: Oxford University Press, 1930.

Raz, S., et al., "The vascular component in the production of intraurethral pressure," *Journal of Urology 108:* 93–96, 1972.

Reis, R. A., and E. J. DeCosta, "Stress incontinence in the female," *American Journal of Obstetrics and Gynecology 53:* 776, 1947.

Sevely, Josephine Lowndes, "Female Ejaculation." Unpublished manuscript, Harvard University, 1976.

Sullerot, Evelyne, *Woman, Society and Change,* trans. by Margaret Scotford Archer. New York: McGraw-Hill, 1971.

Trilling, Lionel, *The Liberal Imagination: Essays on Literature and Society.* New York: Harcourt Brace Jovanovich, 1979.

Yamada, Katsuyoshi, "On the sensory nerve terminations in clitoris in human adult," *Tohoku Journal of Experimental Medicine 54(2):* 1951, pp. 163–174.

Yokochi, Chihiro, and Johannes W. Rohen, *Photographic Anatomy of the Human Body.* Baltimore: University Park Press; Tokyo: Igaku-Shoin, 1978.

INDEX

INDEX

INDEX

PERMISSIONS ACKNOWLEDGMENTS

Figures

1   Courtesy of The Harvard University Art Museums (The Fogg Art Museum) Bequest—Grenville L. Winthrop: studies of a man and a woman, from "The Golden Age" by Jean Auguste-Dominique Ingres (1780–1867).

2   Francis A. Countway Library of Medicine: human vagina, from *Fabrica* (1543) by Andreas Vesalius (1514–1564).

3   Urban & Schwarzenberg GmbH.: erectile bodies of penis, from *Atlas of Human Anatomy,* Vol. 1, 10th Engl. ed.: head, neck, upper extremities; Vol. 2, 10th Engl. ed.: thorax, abdomen, pelvis, lower extremities, skin, 1983 by Johannes Sobotta.

6   Francis A. Countway Library of Medicine: female genitals, adapted from illustrations by Robert Latou Dickinson.

7, 25   Reproduced with permission from Jocelyn & Setchell. H. D. Jocelyn and B. P. Setchell, trans. *Journal of Reproduction and Fertility,* Supplement 17, 1972, from *On the Human Reproductive Organs: Treatise Concerning the Generative Organs of Women,* by Regnier deGraaf, 1672.

9, 10   Credits to CIB for illustrations of the female and male urethras are on pages 29 and 30.

11, 13, 15   S. Karger AG, Basel: illustrations of adult and neonate female urethra, in *Contributions to Gynecology and Obstetrics,* Vol. 10, 1983, from "Aspects of the Anatomy of the Female Urethra with Special Relation to Urinary Continence" by A. B. Huisman.

12   Oxford University Press: illustration of human neonate male urethra (cross section of penis), from *Histology: A Text and* Atlas, 1974, by Johannes A. G. Rhodin.

14   From Sobotta/Hammersen: *Histology: A Color Atlas of Microscopic Anatomy* (Baltimore-Munich: Urban & Schwarzenberg 1985).

Figures

About the Author

JOSEPHINE LOWNDES SEVELY was born in New York City. She married the architect Marvin Sevely and worked with him in his practice, which took them to London, Cairo, and Ankara. For a number of years they lived in New Orleans, where she raised her family and took her B.A. at Newcomb College, Tulane University. Later she did graduate study in psychology and social relations at Harvard University, where she carried out innovative, interdisciplinary research concerning the sexuality of women, a summary of which was subsequently published in the *Journal of Sex Research.* She went on to develop further studies of human female urogenital anatomy and physiology at Brigham and Women's Hospital, a teaching affiliate of Harvard Medical School. One of the objectives of her present work as a medical researcher is to help bring about a closer integration of gynecology and psychology.